‘This is a deeply restorative and strengthening book, that reveals a loving God meeting us in the painful places of our lives. With pastoral wisdom and gentle wit, Jane invites readers to soften barriers around their hearts, souls and minds, allowing God, the wonderful counsellor, to enter their pain and bring genuine healing. For anyone who carries wounds from life’s journey, these pages offer medicine for the soul.’
**Benny Marrett, church leader, Christ Community Church, Attleborough**

‘Honest and gentle, *Give Me Strength!* is written by someone who has been through tough times and, by God’s grace, has come through them and learnt valuable lessons from them. While Jane doesn’t pretend to understand everyone’s circumstances, she offers practical tools that are rooted in scriptural truths and applicable to a wide range of struggles and pain. I would describe this book as a life jacket rather than a lifeboat – helping us to find our way through the pain and to grow stronger as a result, rather than to seek rescue from the storms. It’s a book to savour and to take time over, and is a powerful vehicle for the Holy Spirit to work in and through the tough stuff that life inevitably throws our way.’
**Nicki Copeland, author and speaker**

‘You know when you read a line that takes your breath away? This book contains some stunning lines. This one is my favourite: “My own pride deferred to this seedling, whose apprentice I surely was.” Near the beginning of the book, a precious truth nestles: God’s fingerprints are on us. I had never seen it that way before. It’s a fitting start to a book which encourages us to be God-sufficient, not self-sufficient. *Give Me Strength!* flips the script from “I need to do everything myself” to “God is here to help”. Between these pages, we meet a God who never walks out. Much of it resonated with me, reflecting truths I have learned from life experience. Whether life has knocked you sideways or not, this book is a guide to freedom in God.’
**Emily Owen, author and speaker**

BRF Ministries
15 The Chambers, Vineyard
Abingdon OX14 3FE
**+44(0)1865 319700 | brf.org.uk**

Bible Reading Fellowship (BRF) is a charity (233280) and company limited by guarantee (301324), registered in England and Wales.

EU Authorised Representative: Easy Access System Europe –
Mustamäe tee 50, 10621 Tallinn, Estonia, **gpsr.requests@easproject.com**

ISBN 978 1 80039 525 1
First published 2026
10 9 8 7 6 5 4 3 2 1 0


Cover illustrated by Ben Bloxham



A catalogue record for this book is available from the British Library.

Printed and bound by CPI Group (UK) Ltd, Croydon CR0 4YY

JANE WALTERS

# Give Me Strength!

## Finding all we need in God

BRF Ministries

# ACKNOWLEDGEMENTS

Writing this book has involved reflecting on a lifetime of journeying with Jesus, and I am so grateful not to have had to walk it alone. There are too many dear friends and companions to mention, but if you're reading this, I mean you!

Roy, I owe so much to you. What a joy it was to read each raw chapter to you and have your thoughtful input. Without you, some of this book wouldn't have made sense. Without you in my life, nothing makes sense either. Thank you for loving me so well.

For reasons of confidentiality, I cannot name my counsellor, who came into my life at the perfect time. You helped me make sense of things I couldn't understand and always pointed me to Jesus. I have thanked you many times before, but there is always reason to do so again.

Many thanks to the entire team at BRF Ministries, who have trusted me with this second book. Your challenges provoked me to go deeper and do better, for which I can only be grateful. I felt in safe, prayerful hands throughout the process. You are lovely to work with!

Above all, I give God all the credit, the honour, and the glory. I would always choose a hard life with him than an easy life without him.

# CONTENTS

SECTION III: GROUP STUDIES

# INTRODUCTION

The inspiration for this book lies in a series of encounters I had across a number of years with people who, in a nutshell, were hurting. I spent hours listening to their stories, empathising with their situations, and bringing them to God in prayer. Not that I have been immune from such difficulties myself; far from it. But I have learned to be utterly grateful to God for leading me through each trial, and then for being able to comfort others with the comfort I had received. Ironically, though, I had no sooner embarked on the writing process than a major crisis hit my family, breaking up our unit in an instant, and plunging me into another deep wilderness experience. Finally, several years on from that, I have fulfilled my intention: to share how we can all draw strength from God through the most testing times.

I make no claim to have all the answers, but I have got a pretty good idea of what some of the questions are. We all ask them as we work through our own areas of pain and suffering.

- What is going on?
- How long have I got to put up with this?
- How on earth can I keep going when…?
- Where is God when I need him?

The wonderful thing is that this is not a self-help book. (Plenty of them exist, and maybe you have read your share.) Why is this 'wonderful'? Because although there are steps we can take which may prove helpful, ultimately we're leaning on God and asking him to make the difference. It is not about learning tips and techniques; in fact, in many ways we can say it is not up to us at all. My firm belief – rooted in what the Bible says and borne out in my own experience – is that God is not only the only one who can help, but the only help we ever need. Our cry of 'Give me strength!' need no longer be one of exasperation but our most sincere prayer for help. That is why, throughout, I am pointing us to God. He is the one with the answers. He is the one who cares incredibly deeply for each of us. His is the only strength we ever need.

## How to use this book

The content is divided into daily sections, each day taking around five minutes to read through. That is not to imply this is any quick fix, though. Just as life's events may have taken their time catching up with us, so we can't expect the remedy to be instantaneous. We can't rush the restoration process. We are worth the effort! So, I would encourage you to take the book at your own pace. Don't feel the relevance of a particular chapter? Move on and find one that better hits the spot. Need to spend a couple more days thinking about something? Take your time. There is no stopwatch.

If at all possible, don't skip over the response sections. While I sincerely hope that what I have written will be of help, ultimately it is our interaction with God that matters. He is longing to connect with us, and the suggestions I have made will hopefully enable that to happen.

The evening reflections are a gentle way of mulling over the day's theme before settling down to sleep. Through them, we are entrusting ourselves once more to God, who delights to watch over us as we lie down and sleep.

Working through this book on our own will encourage deeper intimacy with God as we seek him over our difficult issues. However, there is no doubt that getting into discussion with others – with its natural opportunities to pray together and offer mutual support – can add another dimension. The set of group studies in the final section of the book offers standalone material, tied into the book's themes, with suggestions on how to best encourage each other.

It has been my privilege to produce this material, and I pray it will be of enormous benefit and blessing to you.

## Suggested songs playlist

Each chapter has a suggested song at the end for further reflection and worship. You can find these songs compiled in a Spotify playlist via this QR code.

## SECTION I

# An honest look at our weakness

# 1

# ARE YOU SITTING COMFORTABLY?

**The righteous cry out, and the Lord hears them; he delivers them from all their troubles. The Lord is close to the broken-hearted and saves those who are crushed in spirit.**
PSALM 34:17–18

**The Lord God said, 'It is not good for the man to be alone. I will make a helper suitable for him.'**
GENESIS 2:18

I expect you might be sitting somewhere comfortable as you read this, if you're anything like me. I usually do my 'quiet times' in bed, propped up against pillows with my Bible and a book I'm working through to hand. Perhaps you're in a favourite chair or even at your desk, settling into your treasured 'me and God' moment, beginning to read with anticipation buzzing.

So far, so good! But be prepared to shift slightly in your seat, because before we can get down to discovering more about what the Bible says about God's strength – how it can help us and how to receive it – we need to admit the uncomfortable truth that we spend most of our time trying to deny.

We are weak.

If you say 'I am weak' out loud – actually out loud – it might feel strange and unfamiliar. I think we have all found ourselves more often saying, 'I'm fine', even when we're feeling terrible. It is such a natural instinct to cover up, to pretend things are different; and it's no real surprise that we do. After all, it has pretty much been the same way from the beginning – at least, from the beginning of where the Bible tells us it all started to go wrong.

To rewind a little, Genesis tells us that God created the world 'very good' – I suspect that is the equivalent of 'perfect' to you and me – with everything exactly as he had pictured it in his mind. Every landscape, every creature, every detail of every aspect was carefully crafted. When it came to humankind, he went the extra mile, it seemed. While he called most things into being with his voice, it says he formed Adam from the dust of the ground, shaping him in such a way that God's fingerprints would have been all over him. It is an amazing image, isn't it? (Even as I think about that, I sense a longing in me for God to be as real right now – for me to sense him so close. Do you?)

What a position to be in! Living face to face with your creator, in charge of the garden around you. Every corner revealing something new; no reason or opportunity for boredom. Yet before Adam even had the chance to notice there was anything missing, God spotted that work would not be enough to satisfy the man, even in that amazing, brand-new, exciting environment. There was no flaw in God's design, and yet there was potential weakness. God saw that Adam had the capacity to be lonely, and set about meeting a need that hadn't yet become a problem.

A parade of creatures made their way past Adam, as he marvelled at each one and gave them a name. Without sin, there was no danger or reason for fear. This was pure delight – a vast menagerie of pets. Yet the weakness remained, and it was time for another plan.

Enter woman, Eve. She captivated Adam from the get-go, and now the two of them could share everything God had created. He met with the pair of them at the close of each day as the temperatures eased and the work was done. Paradise indeed.

The horror of what happened next is all-too familiar. God's enemy, Satan, sidled into this idyll, his tongue laced with half-truth and insinuation. He put doubt and suspicion in the young wife's mind and the inevitable happened: Eve took the forbidden fruit, ate it, offered it to Adam, and their fate was sealed. Sin had entered the world and, along with it, came an emotion God had never planned for us to feel: shame – that horrible sensation that creeps in and pervades our whole system of feeling 'less than', of waiting for punishment to fall, for us to be found out. It is no surprise that shame makes us want to run and hide – even from (especially from) God. Oh yes, some of us know that feeling only too well.

Sin's corruption of the 'very good' is the source of all that instinct to cover up, hide, deny, and pretend. We might not use fig-leaves as the original humans did, but we all have things we turn to in our attempts to look fine. And this is something that I want us to appreciate, here in chapter 1. There's a sense in which we are all in this together. The Bible tells us that 'all have sinned and fall short of the glory of God' (Romans 3:23). It's a gloomy verse, but focus on the 'all'. You see, when we are going through difficult times, we can so easily believe that we are the only ones who are. Everyone around us might look as though they have it all together, but I can assure you that many of them are pretending. Sadly, even in church.

But, just as we all know what it is to suffer, so we can all know the remedy: God wants to be our strength. Not just 'give us strength', as the title of this book has it; but that he himself would be our strength – his life flowing through our veins is the thing that makes the difference. As surely as he breathed through Adam's nostrils so that the clay man became a living human being, so he can revive us through the Holy Spirit and bring us into new life.

Does this bring hope today? Even a tiny glimmer?

God never intended us to live without his presence and without all he can offer. I think that is why some of our difficulties can feel so very hard: because we weren't designed to experience them. It is true that we are born vulnerable. We are not like other animals who are up on their feet within minutes of birth and learning how to hunt within weeks. Our complete dependence on our parents, particularly our mother, is something that can linger. But even when we develop motor skills and intelligence and even wisdom, it should not be with the aim of becoming self-sufficient. Independence from our parents is a natural part of maturing; but self-reliance was never in God's original blueprint.

Much of what this book sets out to do is to shift our perspective, so that we begin to see our situation through God's eyes instead of our own, which are influenced so much by what our culture teaches us. We are surrounded by the message that to be successful, we need to be stronger, better, richer, faster. The bottom line is that we end up on a kind of hamster wheel, furiously trying harder, running but not getting anywhere. No wonder we end up exhausted.

Thankfully, God's ways are not like our ways. He certainly calls us into purpose, as he did to Adam, commissioning him to tend the garden and be fruitful; but it was never meant to be about striving. As we shall continue to see throughout this book, God is compassionate towards our weakness and frailty. He understands. Our 'stuff' matters to him. And I believe he still wants to walk with us each day, listening to our highs and lows, as he used to in a garden long ago.

We are weak and that can change.

He is strong and will never change.

## Response

Spend some time quietly before God, letting your guard down and taking off those ill-fitting fig-leaves. You are safe here.

What do you need to say to him right now? Write it down if it's easier than speaking it out. Do you sense his reply?

For further reflection and worship, listen to 'Thank God I do' by Lauren Daigle.

## Evening reflection: Tottering steps

*I saw a kid once,*
*I mean an actual baby goat,*
*newly delivered,*
*covered in slime,*
*its mother's mess still on the straw.*
*The kid needed some serious cleaning up*
*and some milk –*
*it was born hungry.*
*No one told it that its legs were weak,*
*their bones, sinews, and muscles untested.*
*Bypassing the science,*
*the kid raised itself on to its feet,*
*tottering and wobbling its way*
*to find its mother,*
*to find help.*
*I'm a kid, too, not newly born*
*but still covered in slime.*
*I still need cleaning up,*
*it's part of my human condition,*
*and despite my best efforts*
*in feeding and tending to myself,*
*I'm still hungry.*
*I know I'm still weak,*
*it's another part of my human condition,*
*and despite my tottering steps*
*and my proneness to be out-of-balance,*
*I'll bypass the theory*
*and keep wobbling my way back*
*to my Father,*
*to find help.*

# 2
# THE WEIGHT OF WEAKNESS

**Praise be to the Lord, to God our Saviour, who daily bears our burdens.**
PSALM 68:19

**'I removed the burden from their shoulders; their hands were set free from the basket.'**
PSALM 81:6

Yesterday, we were looking at Adam and Eve, remembering that God didn't intend us to be alone and looking at the ways sin makes us want to hide. I also emphasised that we are all in this together, so that none of us need feel isolated while we're having such a tough time. It's really important we grasp hold of that truth. Life is hard enough without us feeling as if we're the only ones going through it.

I wonder what effect saying 'I am weak' had yesterday. As I write this, I'm saying those three words too, out loud and over and over.

'I am weak.'

'I am weak.'

'I am weak.'

It's easy enough to say them, but what they mean has powerful implications that go much deeper. Here are my observations on my own response – and some are surprising.

My first feeling was one of a heavy weight landing on me. 'I am weak' came with a deep sense of 'I am a failure'. It may not be the same for all of us, which goes to show how our inner monologue can be a powerfully negative one. I remember one of my music pupils in primary school reporting me to the head teacher. As soon as I arrived the next week, I was met with: 'M is very upset. She says you called her rubbish at the flute.' I was horrified, and instantly felt ashamed and embarrassed. I frantically scrolled back in my mind to the previous week's lesson. I remembered she'd been having trouble getting a particular note, but I would never speak to a pupil the way she described. At last it dawned on me – or perhaps God gave me insight. In trying to help her and correct her, she had obviously been aware that the rest of the group weren't having the same struggles. Compared to them, she felt rubbish. It's what her own heart was saying, and that's what she was listening to. I hadn't said any such thing, nor would I ever have done, but I hadn't needed to for the condemning message to be heard.

I recommend that whenever we become aware of what our heart is saying, we write it down, so we can bring it to God later.

The second time I say, 'I am weak', I'm surprised by a sense of hopelessness. I'm sure I'm not alone in getting through life by working hard and trying harder. Commitments are demanding; we get tired; we have to push through, regardless of how we feel. It can be exhausting. Remembering that, I tune into myself again. Was it really hopelessness? No, perhaps not quite that. It feels more like resignation, actually – not giving up but giving in: admitting, 'Yes, I'm tired and I'm weak.' I'm getting my little white flag ready to wave.

The third time I say it, I'm aware of a welcome sense of peace. It's come because of the surrender, I think. 'I'm weak. I can't do it all. I shouldn't even keep trying. After all, isn't that why Jesus came? To rescue me from all "this"?'

This thought process I've described is typical of the pattern we find in many of the psalms. There is the honest stating of woe, along with a bit of complaining, all of it accompanied by a fixation on what is wrong. The expression of it all, though, makes space for some necessary heart- and soul-searching, too, until finally the psalmist's perspective shifts. He remembers who God is and why he is in our lives. Peace returns.

So often, we want to bypass some of the steps to get more quickly to a result. For example, I want to get fit, but honestly can't be bothered doing all the daily steps or anything. I want to learn how to paint but want to be Monet by the first weekend and preferably on my first attempt. I want to receive God's strength, right here, right now, just by praying the right words. Sadly, that isn't the way it works. And before we can get through to a greater understanding of God's strength and how we can plug into it, we have to do the groundwork regarding our weakness. By which I mean: we need to be honest.

In this private space, this 'me and God' time, we don't need to hold on to 'I'm fine'. In fact, it's essential that we don't. Why not express that with a gesture right now? Maybe like we're throwing it away or dusting it off ourselves. Let's loosen those gritted teeth, lower those tense, raised shoulders. Already we may be sensing some relief. Isn't it ironic that we use up so much energy on the pretence, the mask, when we're already so tired? One of the reasons for that extreme tiredness is that all of what we're describing – whatever those things are – is acting like a huge burden or load that we end up lugging around everywhere with us.

A few years ago, I sensed God unexpectedly nudging me to lay my interior design business down. I'd set up the company seven years earlier and loved the work – even the messy jobs that most people hate doing. That sensing of God's fresh direction took the form of a picture. I imagined myself at the turnstile of a museum or art gallery – one of those fancy places where they don't like you having a rucksack on or whatever. As I made to go through, the attendant stopped me, saying, 'You can't come in here with those,' and he pointed towards the heavy bags I carried in each hand.

A few days later, a friend got in touch. 'I had a dream,' she told me. 'You were carrying two huge supermarket bags, and I felt God say you were to put them down.'

At the time, I took a couple of things from that. First, whatever God had in store for me, I couldn't enter into while I was still hanging on to so much other stuff. And, second, the way ahead was a special place, one that needed protecting. It was all I could do not to look for that 'turnstile' in the excitement of wanting to burst through it.

Looking back, though, I see something else at play. At the time God urged me to lay those 'bags' down, they didn't even feel like they were a problem. I loved my job. Sure, it was tiring, but the occasional exhaustion was worth it. Wasn't it?

The point is that God always knows best. His perspective is perfect; he has 20:20 vision. And, frankly, if he suggests that something in our lives is causing a problem, we would do well to agree with him, even if we see it differently.

Perhaps we know what it is that's weakening us, wearing us out.

Perhaps we'd love someone to point it out for us or, better still, offer to take it from us.

The great news is that Jesus holds the answer in both cases.

It's time to gratefully surrender.

## Response

As you sit quietly, reflecting on these thoughts, take a few deep breaths and let yourself be aware of what is going on in your mind and body.

Is there tension anywhere?

Is there a sense of heaviness that you can pinpoint?

Now imagine that you don't have to feel any of that burden anymore – and turn it into prayer.

*Loving God, I confess that I am weak. The efforts of pretending I am not are making me tired. Please come. Lift the burdens from my shoulders – let me feel the lightness instead of the heaviness. Help me trust that this is good because you are good. Amen.*

For further reflection and worship, listen to 'Strong' by Anne Wilson.

## Evening reflection: Lifting the burden

*'Here, let me…'*
*I register the kind eyes,*
*their hands already assuming my consent,*
*but I shake my head,*
*look away.*
*'No need…'*
*'Just one, then…?'*
*I feel them tug at the handle*
*but still refuse.*
*'They're balanced, it's okay…'*
*I trudge on, more weary than before.*
*Balanced?*
*Honestly?*
*As if my one burden was*
*halved through my body's teamwork?*
*Isn't it more that I'm twice burdened?*
*That's the truth of it,*
*a full load in each hand.*
*I barely know how I'm still upright.*
*One more step,*
*then another.*
*'Help me, God!'*
*'I tried…'*
*'Then try again! Please?'*

# 3

# KNOWING WHO WE ARE DEALING WITH

**And God said, 'I will be with you. And this will be the sign to you that it is I who have sent you: when you have brought the people out of Egypt, you will worship God on this mountain.' Moses said to God, 'Suppose I go to the Israelites and say to them, "The God of your fathers has sent me to you," and they ask me, "What is his name?" Then what shall I tell them?' God said to Moses, 'I AM WHO I AM. This is what you are to say to the Israelites: "I AM has sent me to you."'**

EXODUS 3:12–14

**Then the Lord came down in the cloud and stood there with him and proclaimed his name, the Lord. And he passed in front of Moses, proclaiming, 'The Lord, the Lord, the compassionate and gracious God, slow to anger, abounding in love and faithfulness...'**

EXODUS 34:5–6

Whenever I meet someone new, I'm keen to let them lead the conversation, but it's not because I'm self-effacing. It's simply this: I know all about me – it's the other person I want to know about. So I end up being all questions, all ears.

I don't know when you were first introduced to Jesus, or heard about God. My testimony is that, aged seven, I was at a Christian camp on the Isle of Wight. One day the call went out: there would be a meeting after dinner where we could learn about Jesus. I'll be honest, I had no idea what it even meant. I only knew that a surge of excitement went through me and I fairly skipped along the corridor, eager to know more.

I gave my young heart to Jesus that week and I wish I could say that he and I were best friends from that point on. The reality was that although I continued to go to church, my family were not Christians, and I really didn't know what to do about 'that decision'. It wasn't until I was almost 14 and on a different summer camp in Keswick with the same organisation that I surrendered my entire life to Jesus – and, this time, everything changed. I had the same reason for the surrender and the change. The preacher that night told the packed hall that Jesus loved us. I believed what he said. Why wouldn't I want to trade my life as I knew it for all that love, both now and for eternity? And how could I not change, faced with knowing what it cost God to make that love available?

At that age, I had no thought of what God might do for me and, mercifully, no awareness of what difficulties I would face as I journeyed through life. I suppose the main focus of my new faith was how to behave. (I had stopped swearing the night I gave my life to Jesus.) I was keen to learn what the Bible had to say about attitudes and actions, but hadn't really considered how important it would be to get to know this God I had given everything to. It turned out that doing so was like mining for gold.

Today's verses are incredibly significant. In them, God is revealing himself in his own words. This isn't someone's opinion of him, complete with distortion, filters, and potentially skewed perspective. This is what God says about himself, and we would do well to take note.

A read-through of Genesis shows us that God had already demonstrated a lot about his character. He was a covenant-making God, promising all kinds of good things to Abraham and his endless descendants. Following him revealed his faithfulness, his ability to forgive and restore. All well and good, we might say, but who actually are you?

It's the question Moses asked, in his attempts at side-stepping the commission God was calling him into. 'If anyone asks, what shall I say?'

The answer came through so profoundly that even today Jews do not spell out his name nor take it properly on their lips.

'I AM.'

Two tiny words, but they convey more than a lifetime of theological study can discover. This is what they mean to me:

- **God exists.** He is real and not a figment of the faith-fuelled imagination.
- **God is present.** He is. He is here, he is now. There will never be a time when anyone can speak of his existence in the past tense.
- **God is with us.** Why did the prophets foretell that the promised Messiah would be called Immanuel? Because that was the entire point of the exercise: it was never going to be enough that God existed at a safe distance. He had to identify with us, be with us, present us with unequivocal, undeniable evidence that 'he is'.

It is entirely possible that we can lose sight of any or all of that when we are going through trials and difficulties. I've certainly heard people ask, in words that are sometimes too choice to be repeatable, 'Where is God in this?' Perhaps you were thinking that yourself only recently. And that's why we need to believe, accept, and lean on some truths that will never age and that will never cease to apply. Because if we had to go through the horrible stuff of life on our own, we'd be in a mess no one could clear up or rescue us from.

In my own personal suffering, which I'll be drawing on in the days to come, I may not have got the answers to my tear-drenched questions. I might not have seen the equivalent of a helicopter winch, despite me endlessly searching the skies for it. But… I have believed that God is still 'I AM'.

He is.

There are times when that has to be enough for now.

The second set of verses are quite extraordinary. This is the Old Testament, remember. Don't people have a problem with 'that' God? You know, with his anger issues and everything? The context is that Moses has been privy to God's presence in a way no one had ever been before. He has been up a mountain for 40 days and nights, just him and God, receiving the ten commandments. There was the horror of the golden calf incident, followed by a reissuing of the stone tablets which Moses had smashed in his anger and frustration. Now Moses asks God if he can see his glory (which begs the question of how much Moses actually saw within that mountain-top cloud).

Although God protects Moses from seeing him – which no one could survive – he does promise to pass by and 'proclaim my name, the Lord, in your presence' (Exodus 33:19). But when this takes place, God does not simply repeat that he is 'I AM'. He gives this exquisite description of who he is: 'The LORD , the LORD , the compassionate and gracious God, slow to anger, abounding in love and faithfulness...'

Take your time here.

Read those words again.

Perhaps you have experienced God as distant lately – as uncaring or impassive. Maybe you have felt punished. These are all entirely natural reactions to present suffering, but they are not founded in the truth of who God says he is.

If there is any hope for us, any way out of our mess, it is in the immutable, never-ending, covenantal love of a compassionate, tender-hearted God.

It's what he told Moses.

It's what he wants us to know, too.

## Response

If the doorbell rang right now, and it was rescue arriving at your doorstep, what would you want it to look like?

Tell God that's what you need. (If you found yourself missing someone significant who used to help you, tell him about that, too.)

Wait in the quietness and listen out for what God says in reply.

But know this: whether you sense him or not, he is with you.

For further reflection and worship, listen to 'The Lord is gracious and compassionate' by Vineyard Worship.

## Evening reflection: Hidden from view

*My soul seeks you, O Lord,*
*with heart-longings only you can fill,*
*restless until I know the satisfaction*
*of finding you.*
*Long gone are our forefathers*
*who believed no one could see you and live*
*(though the few brave enough to ask*
*were blessed with a glimpse of your glory).*
*In Jesus, all the fullness of God dwells*
*and when we have seen him,*
*we have seen the Father.*
*And yet…*
*At times, the cloud persists*
*keeping him hidden from view –*
*not the cloud of old which heralded his presence,*
*that spoke of his nearness,*
*but that of my self-generated, self-obsessed*
*doubt and confusion.*
*Are you there, God?*
*I believe you are,*
*so would you come, in blazing radiance,*
*and burn through the swirling mist*
*and make yourself plain?*
*For my soul seeks you, O Lord,*
*with heart-longings only you can fill,*
*restless until I know the satisfaction*
*of finding you.*

# 4
# LITTLE BY LITTLE

**Cast all your anxiety on him because he cares for you.**
1 PETER 5:7

You may be reading this book because you have suffered one of life's body blows. Perhaps it came out of nowhere, caught you off-guard, rendered you incapacitated. Even now, a while after it happened, your heart begins to beat that little bit quicker at the merest thought of it – not that those thoughts are ever far away.

Or maybe there isn't anything you can quite pinpoint as the trigger. In fact, there are some days when you feel almost embarrassed at not having a major crisis at the heart of your troubles. If that's the case, I can tell you now that there's nothing to be ashamed of. As we'll see today (although I suspect you already know), sometimes it's a whole load of little things that do great damage.

It was Eleanor Roosevelt who said, 'A woman is like a teabag: you never know how strong it is until it's in hot water.' The message behind this is one of resilience: when life is tough, it's time to be tougher, to prove you are more than a match for whatever is coming your way. It all sounds admirable, but it's sound bites like this which make it even harder when you find yourself unable to cope. Not only has 'the thing' happened to you, but you are simply not up to the task of dealing with it. You are 'less than'. Too weak. A bit pathetic, really. Does that sound horribly familiar?

When my dad died, initially I coped pretty well. I loved him, for sure, but he was a reserved man and we hadn't had what you could call an emotional connection. At the time, I was working as a peripatetic music teacher, spending my weekdays travelling from school to school. I didn't realise how much of that had become a performance until I returned after the Christmas holidays, some seven months after my bereavement. I heard myself say, 'Hello everyone! So how was your Christmas?' in my usual cheery way. The shock was that my words sounded and felt utterly hollow. It was like I had gone on stage without wearing a costume. Suddenly, I was a fake. I couldn't do it anymore.

A visit to my GP had me diagnosed with clinical depression and signed off from work for two weeks, which I interpreted as a target: I had two weeks to get myself better. I phoned my boss to let him know. 'Sorry to hear that, strawberry,' he said – having never referred to me as fruit before, 'You're strong. You'll soon bounce back.'

I believed him. It's what I'd been telling myself.

Except that we were both wrong. I wouldn't be well enough to return to work for another 18 months.

If I were standing in front of you now and asked you to pick up a huge, heavy box, I would expect you to refuse, for very good reason. It's too big, too heavy, too awkward. You don't need me; you need a crane.

Or what if I asked you to hold your hands out as I proceeded to transfer objects on to you from a huge pile? You might manage the first few, once you've shifted your arms and feet a bit. But it wouldn't be long before something dropped from your grasp, followed by another as you leaned over to stop the avalanche. If I still kept on with the loading, you would be telling me to stop and moving yourself out of my reach.

The trouble is, of course, that the things that burden us aren't generally as obvious as that. I've lost count of the times I've picked something up – a responsibility, usually – considering it to be perfectly manageable, only to realise that there was a hidden weight to it or that I had a hidden weakness. If we could somehow see the physical dimensions, we would probably make better decisions.

And what of those multiple things we try to carry? In my experience, too many of them seem to have our name on them. Common sense tells us it's way too much for one person, but if we don't try to carry them, who will? Single parents don't have much choice. Nor do carers. Nor those with any kind of sickness or disability, whether long- or short-term. So we continue to find a way through: by 'dropping the ball' in sometimes key areas; or cutting back on sleep or rest, threatening our physical and mental well-being even further; or neglecting relationships because we simply don't have the capacity.

My line manager had predicted that I would bounce. Perhaps you've thought that you would, too. In fact, my mental health broke, and it didn't do my physical well-being any good, either, as my weight went up by two stones. But here's the thing: God didn't create us to bounce, and he never intended us to break. No. His plan all along was that we should be carried. Let's explore some scripture verses in pursuit of this idea.

> **Even to your old age and grey hairs I am he, I am he who will sustain you. I have made you and I will carry you; I will sustain you and I will rescue you.**
> ISAIAH 46:4

I wonder which words leaped out at you first? It's usually an indication of where our focus is or our deepest need. The fact is, each phrase is astonishing. When you consider how the world views God as either non-existent, or distant, or irrelevant, here he is portrayed as involved intimately with us from the moment he created us to the moment we die. I remember the relief when my 18-month-old son, of solid proportions, finally worked out that he could walk and I didn't have to lug him around anymore. God is never like that with us. In fact, we are more likely to be squirming within his grasp, eager to be off on our own, than he is to let us go.

This promise of him carrying us, sustaining us, and rescuing us has no sell-by date. There's no sense that he cares in this way only until we're strong enough to be able to manage without him. Our weakness, our inability to be entirely self-sufficient, gives him the delightful opportunity to offer us tender compassion – again and again and again.

> **'You yourselves have seen what I did to Egypt, and how I carried you on eagles' wings and brought you to myself.'**
> EXODUS 19:4

This illustration of strength and power – and of lifting us high above the earth's surface and all its difficulties – is made more personal in a similar reminder.

> **'The Lord your God, who is going before you, will fight for you, as he did for you in Egypt, before your very eyes, and in the wilderness. There you saw how the Lord your God carried you, as a father carries his son, all the way you went until you reached this place.'**
> DEUTERONOMY 1:30–31

'All the way you went...'

'Even to your old age...'

Let those truths sink in.

No matter what burdens we carry, and however long we have been trying to bear them, God wants to bring us relief. He wants to lift us, to hold us, to carry us away from where we are now – and we will never, ever, be too much for him.

## Response

Imagine yourself standing and there are huge arms around you.

When you go to pick up that heavy burden, it is weightless because those enveloping arms are doing the work.

Those multiple items you keep dropping? God's voice whispers in your ear, 'I've got this.'

Take a few minutes to let peace seep into you at the thought that life could look and feel like this. If you feel able, you could pray:

*Please let it be like this for me, God. Don't be far away. I need you now.*

For further reflection and worship, listen to 'Burdens' by Jamie Kimmett.

## Evening reflection: The unburdening

*The day is done*
*and my mind is wearied*
*by its constant buzzing,*
*my heart from its incessant caring.*
*I breathe more deeply –*
*'Slow, my soul, slow;*
*it's time to let go,*
*let go.'*
*I feel my shoulders drop with relief*
*as the weight of a thousand burdens*
*falls away and I*
*kick them out of reach.*
*'Slow, my soul, slow;*
*it's time to let go,*
*let go.'*
*And with footsteps soft behind me*
*comes my Saviour, right on cue.*
*Mind stilled, heart loosed,*
*I am free to embrace him.*
*'Slow, my child, slow;*
*I'll never let go,*
*let go.'*

# 5

# DIMINISHED BY DISAPPOINTMENT

**Hope deferred makes the heart sick...**
PROVERBS 13:12

**Take delight in the Lord, and he will give you the desires of your heart.**
PSALM 37:4

'Disappointment: Non-fulfilment of an expectation, intention, or desire' – *Oxford English Dictionary*.

What is it about the word 'disappointment'? Whether I write it, think it, or say it, the effect is the same: it lands like a weight on my heart.

The reason is all too obvious: it's not just a word, a collection of letters that we may not even be able to spell right. Rather, it's a reminder, a trigger even, of a whole host of events and situations that have left a horrible imprint and a bitter aftertaste.

We have considered already the cumulative effect that some things have on us. Some of us might be dealing with a massive disappointment right now, a kind of body blow that leaves us breathless and reeling. For others – and I put myself in this category – it feels like life is too often a let-down. People, situations, whatever and wherever the disappointment strikes, there's a sense of 'Again? Really?' Both the acute and the chronic experiences have similar effects, which we will explore today before looking at what can be done about it.

One of the first instincts is to hide our disappointment – yet another opportunity for us to wear a mask. Even children learn to do this, to squash it down, for fear of hurting someone else. That present you didn't really like? Put on a smile, and say it's just what you wanted. That event you didn't win or the job you failed to secure? Congratulate them, tell them it was well-deserved, that you're glad to have lost out to such a worthy candidate. We've all done it. I suspect, though, that the feelings we buried are still in there and having effects somewhere. Do you sense that it's probably time to unearth them and deal with them properly?

Painful though it is, we simply must be honest – at least with ourselves – and allow the feelings to bubble up. This will take courage. Too often we can be afraid of lifting the lid on our emotions, believing that their freedom will wreak havoc, that we won't be able to regain control. It's understandable to feel like that, but that fear also keeps us stuck. Remember why you are reading this book: because you are looking for something to change, to improve. Don't lose sight of that goal.

Part of this honesty is confessing the conclusions we've drawn from repeated disappointment: that we're not important to other people, that our stuff doesn't matter, and that God doesn't care about us enough. Sound familiar? Let's unpack some of that. (By the way, do take time to pause while reading all this, to let your feelings catch up with your thinking.)

*'I'm not important to other people.'* Actually, digging into that only a little way reveals something just under the surface: we believe that being treated well is part of being loved. So, when we are overlooked or don't get what we believe we need, we're actually taking that to mean that we are not loved. It might seem quite a leap, but for us, with our skewed perspectives and our stack of corroborating evidence, it's a small step we can make every time even the slightest disappointment comes our way.

*'My stuff doesn't matter.'* This is the conclusion that originally led me into getting some counselling. I was living in a very difficult situation, one which took a lot of emotional juggling and, at times, what felt like survival skills. 'It doesn't matter' was a phrase I said to myself so often over a period of years that in the end I realised the side effect to this position of attempted safety was that I couldn't feel anything at all. Just as anaesthetised skin shows no reaction to a pin prick, my poor heart learned how to block out every stimulus. I felt less pain, true, but I felt less everything. Nothing was funny or sad anymore. Nothing mattered. I was entirely numb.

*'God doesn't care about me enough.'* That's a big one, isn't it? If you've thought it at all, what voice are you using? Is it a whisper in the dark? Spat out in anger? Said with a shrug? God sees and knows it all. The psalmist models being honest with him: 'Listen, Yahweh, to my passionate prayer! Can't you hear my groaning? Don't you hear how I'm crying out to you?' (Psalm 5:1–2, TPT). There is real desperation here, and an expectation that God is going to listen (however distant he seems) and do something about it. I think it's the desperation that God takes notice of, more than the words. There's a danger, though, in concluding that God doesn't care: it acts as an off-switch to our communication with him. Our internal motto becomes something like, 'What's the point?'

Can you see where these (legitimate and natural) thoughts take us? Whether we're saying, 'I don't matter', 'It doesn't matter', or 'God doesn't care', we're demonstrating a lack of hope. We didn't notice it as we stepped on to this path, but that's where the signpost was pointing. Every step collects more despair to our souls and can end up bogging us down entirely.

But before we become disappointed about ever getting free of disappointment, it's time to lift our faces up to the light and let God do something about it.

At the root of disappointment, as the dictionary makes clear, is an unmet expectation. All our negative emotions and responses spring from this initial trigger. My friend didn't follow through with their promised invitation. My boss promoted the other person in my department. It rained all through our summer holiday. It will be easy for each of us to fill in our own blanks, since there are many of them. Sometimes it's possible to see that our expectations were a bit off: that friend has never been reliable; I really messed up that interview. But on other occasions, our expectations were valid and justified, yet it still didn't work out. It hurts; it really does.

Here's where we have to be resolute in our response. Sadly, there's nothing we can do about the disappointing situation, because it has already happened. The answer isn't to toughen up and harden our hearts. It's better that we choose to be honest about how it has affected us, letting the emotions out instead of allowing them to fester. There's a reason they call it 'bitter disappointment'. We don't want to be the sort of people who allow bitterness to pervade our hearts and character. It always ends up showing.

Once the crying, complaining, shouting, or whatever else is done – which could take a very long time – a peace descends. All that negative emotion has been taking up a lot of internal space, and God has been poised to flood us with peace and contentment instead. Use these still moments to surrender to God. He has seen everything that has happened, even the behind-the-scenes action we haven't been privy to. We can be sure he has wept for and over us. Every time we have said fiercely, 'It doesn't matter', there has been an echo from heaven that asserted, 'It matters to me.'

Like any burden that weighs us down and saps our strength, the best thing to do is lay it down. It is too heavy for us to bear. Jesus is waiting for us to hand it over to him. We don't have to worry about the theology; we just need to let it go. That's enough for now. We'll be starting to talk about hope tomorrow.

## Response

God wants to lift disappointment from us, so we no longer have to bear its burden.

In a physical gesture, offer the weight of it to God, thanking him for how much you matter to him.

*Take it, Lord. Take it all! Amen.*

For further reflection and worship, listen to 'Firm foundation (He won't)' by Cody Carnes.

## Evening reflection: Here, let me

*Let down again, for the millionth time:*
*ironic that the only thing that doesn't disappoint is*
*disappointment itself.*
*It's sure to turn up even when the good stuff stays home.*
*Yet again, I feel its weight,*
*pressed somewhere under my ribs*
*or in the pit of my stomach.*
*But then a new truth steps forward,*
*thrusts out a hand in introduction.*
*Ah yes, we met only today,*
*remind me of your name?*
*Hope, the truth says,*
*pleased to meet you.*
*Here, let me…*
*And I find I offer no resistance*
*as Hope takes from me the stack of boxes,*
*each one labelled, 'The time when…'*
*I look down at my empty arms,*
*suddenly light, and my heart with them,*
*and smile.*

# 6

# WHAT IS OUR HOPE ROOTED IN?

**We remember before our God and Father your work produced by faith, your labour prompted by love, and your endurance inspired by hope in our Lord Jesus Christ.**
1 THESSALONIANS 1:3

**Let us hold unswervingly to the hope we profess, for he who promised is faithful.**
HEBREWS 10:23

There's an odd comfort in difficulty. Somewhat out of keeping in a book such as this, the phrase that comes to mind is 'Better the devil you know'. It's something I witnessed in a friend's father many years ago. He had been in a wheelchair for many years, having had a bad accident at work, and although I'm not sure how deep his faith went, he used to go to church most weeks. When I asked my friend why his dad didn't go up for healing prayer, his answer surprised me: 'He's used to it now. It would be too difficult to adjust back to normal life.'

Another story springs to mind, this time from the Bible. A paralysed man is at the healing pool of Bethesda, waiting for the moment the waters are agitated, signalling the possibility of a miracle. 'When Jesus saw him lying there and learned that he had been in this condition for a long time, he asked him, "Do you want to get well?"' (John 5:6). It's not such a strange question, given that the man has been waiting there like that for 38 years! His answer betrays what has been going on in his heart: '"Sir," the invalid replied, "I have no one to help me into the pool when the water is stirred. While I am trying to get in, someone else goes down ahead of me"' (v. 7).

When we're faced with difficulty and its attendant disappointments, it's very easy for resignation to creep in. Perhaps we began in good heart: understanding that God leads us through valleys as well as up mountains, trusting him to lead us on, believing him for better things. But as we tried to stand strong, we got tired and, yes, disillusioned too. Our prayers seemed to go unanswered and those situations didn't look like they were changing anytime soon. No wonder that little spark of hope gets smothered. Like the paralysed man at the pool, it might look like we're still fighting, still trying, but there goes that inner motto again, repeating, 'What's the point?'

In other words, hope has gone.

Despair has arrived in its place – and it has no bright side we can look on.

Just as disappointment and the other problems we face creep up on us without us knowing, so hope gradually slinks wordlessly away. It's only when it's gone do we realise what lay behind our 'mojo', our reason to get up in the morning. Hope is what keeps us trying, even when it's not going well. Hope has us trusting that we'll get there in the end, that everything will work out. Hope has us saying things like, 'Every cloud has a silver lining', and hope makes us believe it.

Some people are natural optimists. We call them 'glass-half-full types'. When faced with a problem, they only seem to see the potential solution – and the excitement of discovering it. Where they see challenges, they don't seem outfaced by them. Hardships come, for sure, but it's not the only thing they talk about. I've drawn a conclusion about such people: either they are delusional and divorced from reality or their hope is rooted in extremely fertile soil. In the case of Christians, I'm pretty sure it's the latter. Let's look at what I mean by that, which involves turning to the Bible.

According to my NIV concordance, the first mention of the word hope in the Bible is when Naomi says, ‘Even if I thought there was still hope for me…’ (Ruth 1:12; we’ll be starting to look at Naomi’s story in chapter 8.) I was expecting the idea to come up sooner, if I’m honest. Perhas, though, it shouldn’t surprise that it wasn’t there right from the beginning. That’s because hope is all about a better future. We bother to hope at all because there’s something lacking in the present. And at the beginning of creation, when Adam and Eve spent idyllic days in the garden of Eden, enjoying God’s company, there was nothing else they needed. Why hope for better days, when the present ones are so sweet? Why worry about what is to come, when day after day the evidence is that nothing could go wrong? We only need hope because of the uncertainties in life, because things don’t always go to plan, because we are not in control. Thankfully, we can have it.

At this point, whatever our feelings, we simply have to look to God. I truly know no other answer for any of life’s troubles than his Son, Jesus. I know of no other words that can cut through the results of Google searches or other people’s opinions or my own defiant viewpoints like his can. How we need the word of God!

> **Yes, my soul, find rest in God; my hope comes from him. Truly he is my rock and my salvation; he is my fortress, I shall not be shaken.**
> PSALM 62:5–6

> **For you have been my hope, Sovereign Lord, my confidence since my youth.**
> PSALM 71:5

> **You are my refuge and my shield; I have put my hope in your word.**
> PSALM 119:114

> **Then you will know that I am the Lord; those who hope in me will not be disappointed.**
> ISAIAH 49:23

It wasn't hard to find scriptures that point to God as the source of hope; and these few can serve to get us started on readjusting our compass, setting our thoughts on him. It's interesting how many other benefits are mentioned once we start seeking hope. Psalm 62 speaks of rest, which we may not naturally associate with hope. Rest comes from being able to lean on God, knowing he can always bear our weight, whether that weight comes from the heaviness in our body, heart, soul, and mind. When we turn to him, in hope that our load may become lighter, we find he not only lifts it from us but offers us deep relief, too. Psalm 71 reminds us that hope can be a lifelong promise. We can put our hope in God and gain hope for our lives again and again, knowing him to be faithful and never fickle. Psalm 119 repeatedly holds up the word of God as the answer for all we need, and in the verse above a reason is given: he is our refuge and shield.

God is light and in him is no darkness at all.

He is love and in him is no indifference at all.

He is hope and in him is no disappointment at all.

There is more to unpack in the coming days, but for now, take this to heart: for all the ways we have been badly disappointed and hurt by our life experiences and the people within them, God has the solution.

Hope.

It's who he is and what he offers.

It can be ours for the taking, for the knowing, for the embracing.

This is truth that can set us free.

## Response

Look again at the scriptures this chapter has highlighted. Which one speaks to you most? Can you rewrite it in your own words, making it apply specifically to your situation?

What message do you think God is trying to convey to you?

*God, life has been so hard for so long that it's hard to think differently. Please let your word be effective in my heart and mind. I want the rest that you promise. I want to know the freedom you won for me on the cross. I want to dare to hope. Amen.*

For further reflection and worship, listen to 'Cornerstone' by Hillsong Live 2012.

## Evening reflection: Find rest, O my soul

*Sounds of day are retreating,*
*their footsteps reduced to a tap-tapping*
*against the cobbles of hours past.*
*Not yet peace*
*not yet night*
*only twilight outside and within.*
*'Find rest, O my soul, in God alone;*
*my hope comes from him.'**
*Anxious thoughts, desist your restless throbbing.*
*Mind, cease your whirring.*
*It's nearly time for sleep –*
*that blessed fleeting coma of respite*
*I have craved since waking.*
*Heart, be still,*
*ease back on your thumping.*
*Tasks are done, if not completed,*
*and tomorrow may bring time enough,*
*or so I pray;*
*so I hope.*
*'Find rest, O my soul, in God alone;*
*my hope comes from him.'*

*Psalm 62:5

# 7

# HOPE AGAINST ALL HOPE

> **Against all hope, Abraham in hope believed and so became the father of many nations, just as it had been said to him, 'So shall your offspring be.' Without weakening in his faith, he faced the fact that his body was as good as dead – since he was about a hundred years old – and that Sarah's womb was also dead. Yet he did not waver through unbelief regarding the promise of God, but was strengthened in his faith and gave glory to God, being fully persuaded that God had power to do what he had promised.**
>
> ROMANS 4:18–21

We began exploring hope yesterday, understanding how much we need it in a world where disappointment and despair are our frequent companions. Perhaps we know some of the theology well enough. Perhaps we've committed to memory some of the great promises in scripture, and can recite them in times of need, but still something is missing. That distance of around 30 centimetres between our brain and our heart can be a gulf as wide as a canyon sometimes. So today, let's take an honest look at how hard it is to stay hopeful when life circumstances rob us of it.

The passage above became a game changer for me during one of the worst seasons of my life.[1] After the birth of my son, which had been, according to my midwife, a textbook experience, I then went on to have four miscarriages. Each one brought its own challenges, emotionally and physically, but it was after the third that I became aware of the spiritual impact. Women in our church were conceiving and then giving birth to their babies. One had a threatened loss but after some bed-rest and lots of prayer, all was well. I was the odd one out. When a friend came round to console me, like Job's comforters she only succeeded in making things worse. To be fair, she tried to quickly back-pedal and reword what she'd said. It was too late, though. I had heard her loud and clear: I obviously hadn't been praying right. It only served to confirm what I feared: it really had been all my fault.

Fast forward a couple of months, and I was staying with friends when the dinnertime conversation turned to the topic of hope. I had nothing to contribute, of course, and excused myself from the table. Once safely in my room, I dropped to my knees and pleaded with God for forgiveness over not being able to hope: 'I want to be able to, Lord, and I'm sorry for my lack of faith; but I just can't see any way forward. My hope has all gone.'

I wonder if you've felt anything like that or can relate in some way? If we were together right now and you told me a story like that, I would be sure to tell you what no one was telling me back then: it's okay. It's perfectly understandable to have reached such a depth of despair when life has sucked for so long. And hear this: we have a God who, in Jesus, knows what hopelessness feels like. There is no need for apology. Simply know that God has so much compassion to offer each of us.

Back then, I felt I was letting God down by my lack of faith and my inability to hope. I thought that if I was going through all this in order to learn a lesson, then it was a class I was failing, big time. Thank God he doesn't think or operate as we do! Instead, through an article in a magazine lent to me by a (much better) friend, I found Romans 4. Dear Abraham! He would go on to become known as a giant of the faith and an esteemed pillar of the Jewish religion, and yet he'd been given a promise that was, frankly, preposterous. To have a child, when all of nature said it couldn't be done? To have so much riding on it when neither he nor his wife had it in them anymore?

'Against all hope, Abraham in hope believed' (Romans 4:18). I liked the sound of that immediately. His situation – and mine – did not carry any hope of its own. In fact, everything was pushing in the opposite direction. And yet… I found something stirring in my heart. I had found a possible doorway.

'Being fully persuaded that God had power to do what he had promised' (v. 21). Yes. I had no hope that I would have another baby, but I did know that God had the power to do what he had promised. It might only have been head-knowledge, but I was sure of it. And in taking hold of this verse, then clutching it tight, I had inadvertently changed the course of not only my thinking but also my believing – because it wasn't too long after that that it slipped its way into my heart.

You see, whatever we are currently going through, and however despairing we have become, there is a truth about hope that we don't (or can't) learn when life is sweet. Hope isn't so much about fixating on a solution or a way out. It isn't even about wanting things to change (though we long for them to do so). The Bible says it clearly:

> **He has brought us by faith into this experience of God's grace, in which we now live. And so we boast of the hope we have of sharing God's glory! We also boast of our troubles, because we know that trouble produces endurance, endurance brings God's approval, and his approval creates hope. This hope does not disappoint us, for God has poured out his love into our hearts by means of the Holy Spirit, who is God's gift to us.**
> ROMANS 5:2–5 (GNB)

At one time, I would have rolled my eyes at that, thinking of all the times that my hope had indeed turned to disappointment, but now I understand better. Hope is rooted far more in God's love for us than it is in our circumstances. We hate going through troubles of any kind; we would much rather have an easy, quiet life. And yet it's not the way God leads us. Above all, he wants to lead us further into his heart. He wants to be the one we turn to first. He wants to be the answer to all our questions. He wants us.

It bears repeating: he wants us.

He wants to lavish his love upon us.

All too often, that involves a tricky and even dangerous route. Paul seems to be saying that holding firm, digging deep, and taking God at his word are all paths towards hope. He didn't say so lightly. He recounts troubles greater than we can imagine (2 Corinthians 11:25; see also Hebrews 11:37) and still considers them worth it for the sake of knowing Jesus better (Philippians 3:10). Job, another example of enduring terrible suffering, asks in his torment: 'Where then is my hope – who can see any hope for me?' (Job 17:15). Perhaps you said something like this only just now. It isn't meant to be a rhetorical, unanswerable question. It is meant to find its answer in God himself.

## Response

Imagine your hope looking like an open fire at the end of the day. The flames have made way for so much ash, ready for clearing out. And yet, if you look closely, there are the tiniest of wisps of smoke. Gently give it a poke. Did you see that glint of red, feel that waft of warm air? Don't strive. Don't try to make anything happen. Just wait.

*God, it really has been feeling like the fire has gone out. It's all been such rubbish for so long. Would you stir hope in me again? Rekindle that spark in my heart? Be the answer I've been searching for, please?*

For further reflection and worship, listen to 'It is well' by Kristene DiMarco.

## Evening reflection: Unless a seed

*I thought the seed had died,*
*so long had it been since*
*I planted it.*
*Every day I watered it –*
*just a sprinkle, not a splash –*
*and watched,*
*and waited.*
*Nothing.*
*Still nothing.*
*Not so much as a break in the soil.*
*So I turned my back on it,*
*that wretched barren pot,*
*and in my anger*
*refused it all attention.*
*Until the morning when on waking*
*I found the room ablaze with the sun*
*and a green shoot,*
*no taller than my fingernail,*
*stood in all its glorious potential.*
*My own pride deferred to this seedling,*
*whose apprentice I surely was.*
*This is hope.*

# 8

# LEARNING FROM NAOMI: TELLING IT LIKE IT IS

> **'It is more bitter for me than for you, because the Lord's hand has turned against me!'**
> RUTH 1:13

Amid the Old Testament records of Israel's turbulent history of endless sinning and repenting lies the book of Ruth. Only four chapters long, we could say it punches above its weight, its charming love story lingering long after the pages are closed. However, it isn't only the story of Ruth catching the eye of the older man who would become her husband. It is also the story of Naomi, a disenchanted, depressed widow, who'd had more knocks than she could withstand. God is no discriminator when it comes to his rescue plan. As we shall see, he doesn't give up on us when we (and others) have given up on ourselves. In our individual, unique ways, he wants us all to live 'happily ever after'.

Naomi came from Bethlehem, many, many generations before its famous baby was to be born. She enjoyed her life being married to Elimelech (let's call him Elim, for short), and facing the usual ups and downs of rearing two sons – until famine hit the land and it was a question of move or die. The decision was made to uproot the family and go into neighbouring Moab 'for a while' (Ruth 1:1). 'It's only temporary,' Elim might have assured his family, 'just until the worst has passed. We'll be back before you know it, you'll see.'

Once there, however, the blows kept coming. Food there may have been, but heartache followed. Elim died, leaving Naomi with her two sons, who each married and established households of their own.

Within ten years, however, both sons also died, meaning Naomi had lost all the men she loved. Her two daughters-in-law were a comfort, but culturally worlds apart at times. How many times did Naomi regret they'd ever gone to Moab?

Finally, news came from Bethlehem: God had heard his people's desperate prayers and the harvest was coming in. Naomi knew it was time to go back. We are not privy to the conversation that took place between her and her sons' widows, but they agreed to make the journey, too. A fresh start was what they all needed. If Naomi had adapted to a foreign climate for the sake of her family, then surely they could do the same for her?

They set out on the rough, mountainous road, with something like ten days' walking ahead of them; but Naomi soon had a change of heart. What had she been thinking of, expecting these two young women to give up everything they knew for the sake of a washed-up, old woman?

> **'Go back, each of you, to your mother's home. May the Lord show you kindness, as you have shown kindness to your dead husbands and to me. May the Lord grant that each of you will find rest in the home of another husband.'**
> RUTH 1:8–9

They refused to hear of any such thing, no doubt clinging to Naomi and assuring her that they were all in this together, that family was everything – whatever it looked like. But Naomi held firm. 'Return home…' What would be the point in them sticking with her, when the likelihood of her finding a new husband was so slim, and the thought of producing more sons for them to marry was both unfeasible and ridiculous.

> **'No, my daughters. It is more bitter for me than for you, because the Lord's hand has turned against me!'**
> RUTH 1:13

Let's just pause in the story there. I know that some of this has been speculation on my part. We can't know for sure how Naomi had dealt with the heartbreak of bereavement, and our own stories can colour our views on others' circumstances. But in a few short verses, we can see what she has gone through and finally our guess-work isn't needed.

> **'The Lord's hand has turned against me!'**

The exclamation mark is barely necessary. This is a woman who has had enough. She set out in hope and faith and it's brought her nothing but trouble. No, more than that. God has brought her nothing but trouble. He has not just ignored her or neglected her, though that would have been bad enough. To her eyes, he has turned against her. There was no need to drag anyone else into it.

Orpah, the older of the 'girls', soon changed her mind. Her tears betray the difficulty of the decision, but stay in Moab she would.

Ruth, however, was a different case. Her tender but fierce words have been quoted so many times through generation after generation.

> **'Don't urge me to leave you or to turn back from you. Where you go I will go, and where you stay I will stay. Your people will be my people and your God my God. Where you die I will die, and there I will be buried. May the Lord deal with me, be it ever so severely, if even death separates you and me.'**
> RUTH 1:16–17

I imagine the look on her face would have sealed the deal. She intended to have the last word, and it seems to have done the trick.

I wonder how much of the journey was made in silence, each of the women lost in their own thoughts. Neither of them would be able to visit their husband's resting place. Neither knew what lay ahead of them. Ruth may have prayed as she walked, but I suspect Naomi did not. Their hearts were as heavy as the packs they carried.

Finally arriving in Bethlehem, the place had changed and so had Naomi. Word quickly got out that she had been spotted – or, at least, someone who looked a bit like her.

'Naomi…?'

Before the enquirer had a chance to ask after her, the answer came back, sharp and definitive:

> **'Don't call me Naomi [meaning 'pleasant'],' she told them. 'Call me Mara [meaning 'bitter'], because the Almighty has made my life very bitter. I went away full, but the Lord has brought me back empty. Why call me Naomi? The Lord has afflicted me; the Almighty has brought misfortune upon me.'**
> RUTH 1:20–21

Bitter.

Empty.

We could add more: hopeless, written off, at the end of her tether.

And, what's more, the blame was laid squarely at God's feet.

Let's pause again.

There's something about Naomi's horrible experiences, and her reactions, that resonates powerfully with our own stories. We don't have to have gone through the same things before we can empathise with someone in their pain. We've all known loss, whether that's people or places, things external or internal. We've known what it is to cry out our woes in front of God or with our friends. We've prayed, with perhaps diminishing reserves of faith, still clinging on to the hope that God might yet come through for us, that something might yet change.

So far, it hasn't paid off.

I get that. I really do. Perhaps you've drawn the same awful conclusions as Naomi about where God is in all this. Perhaps you haven't quite dared.

We'll go on tomorrow to look at more of Naomi's story, which gets better, I'm glad to say. But, for today, take Naomi's hand – as Ruth did – and make the same pledge not to go anywhere. It might not feel like it, but God is not very far away, looking on.

## Response

Sit quietly with whatever thoughts and feelings have been stirred by today's reading.

Don't be tempted to rush on, however much you want to avoid thinking.

If you need help knowing what to pray, use these words:

*God, life has been so awful. Even starting to think about it is overwhelming. Bring me through this, please. I want to believe you still care for me, even though you didn't stop it happening. I want to believe you can strengthen me. Amen.*

For further reflection and worship, listen to 'Oceans' by Hillsong United, cover by Genavieve Linkowski.

## Evening reflection: Another day done

*How can I put into words*
*what silence might better say?*
*Surely the sound of my sighing*
*conveys well enough the ache in my soul?*
*So much has gone wrong*
*too much to endure.*
*Another day of coping –*
*well, trying to –*
*brings me to my knees,*
*not in worship*
*but despair.*
*A voice from the past begins to whisper:*
*'Gentle Jesus, meek and mild,*
*look upon this little child.*
*Pity my simplicity*
*suffer thee to come to me.'*[2]
*Let this ancient bedtime prayer*
*be mine once more,*
*soothing my soul.*
*(Can it be? Lord?)*
*I need your pity, your compassion,*
*your free-flowing mercy*
*to not only draw me to you*
*but hold me tight*
*through this night*
*and always.*

# 9

# LEARNING FROM NAOMI: THE WEIGHT OF REGRET

**'The Lord has afflicted me; the Almighty has brought misfortune upon me.'**
RUTH 1:21

**Because of the Lord's great love we are not consumed, for his compassions never fail.**
LAMENTATIONS 3:22

We left Naomi yesterday at the height – or, better, the depth – of her troubles. She was starting the miserable job of settling back into her hometown, among familiar places and people yet so altered inside herself. Every street she walked, every person she saw, must have been a reminder of what she had lost.

*It's all gone. Look at them all, carrying on as if nothing has changed! That's right, stare all you like. I don't care anymore…*

Speculation, I know, but it's easy to imagine.

It's a painful truth that we sometimes have to carry the weight of the consequences of our actions. Naomi's husband had made the decision to move his family into the next country, setting off a chain of events that irrevocably changed Naomi's life. Did she have a choice in the matter? Did she question (again and again) why she'd allowed herself to be persuaded to go along with it? Would everything have been alright if only they had stayed put? All we can surmise with confidence is that she must have regretted their decision.

Joni Eareckson Tada was only 17 years old when she dived into shallow water in Chesapeake Bay and broke her neck. Years later, she could describe the dive as 'reckless', but at the time she was confident in her youth and her athleticism, believing she could quickly straighten out from the intended back pike and come right up out of the water again. Instead, she immediately hit the sea floor, forcing her head back and leaving her paralysed from the shoulders down.

As a teenager, I read her early books *Joni* and *A Step Further*, where she described her battles with depression as she wrestled to accept her lot. Understandably so. In researching for today's chapter, I read more recent articles and watched video clips of her, more than half a century on. I came across this wonderful anecdote, describing an event at one of Joni's charities supporting the disabled, where around 3,500 people had gathered:

> A college-aged volunteer approached me, holding a kid with Down syndrome on her hip. She gestured at the crowd and asked, 'Miss Joni, do you ever think how none of this would be happening were it not for your diving accident?' I flashed a smile and said, 'It's why I thank God every day for my wheelchair'.[3]

She made it sound so simple, so sorted – a testament to what God can do when a person yields their life to him. But then I watched a 2023 video clip where she describes what happened back in 1967 and saw her eyes well with tears at the recollection. Whatever battles she has overcome, boy, have they been hard-won. I heard her regret over that fateful decision that summer's day. She describes how she had only recently, back then, prayed a prayer of absolute surrender to God, saying, 'Jesus, do something in my life to really grip it up. Do anything in my life it's gonna take to draw me close to you. I want that. I need that.' And then, soon afterwards, she broke her neck. She concluded, 'I thought that God could never be trusted with a prayer again.'[4]

Joni's example is an extreme one, but it acutely highlights how the consequences of our actions are sometimes incredibly tough to bear.

Why didn't we see what was coming – what would happen if we said or did that thing? How come we didn't play it forward with enough wisdom or insight, so we could have acted differently, spared ourselves and others such pain? It's one of the facts of our human condition, one of the symptoms of our imperfection and weakness, that we find ourselves in that position more often than we would like. Édith Piaf famously sang that she regretted nothing (was that irony or bravado?), but I doubt any of us could genuinely say the same.

I wonder what decisions you regret.

How many of them have locked you into a situation you feel there is no escape from?

It might be appropriate to lay the book to one side and just sit with those thoughts for a moment or two.

Let's return to Naomi, weighed down by all that had gone wrong since leaving for Moab. It is tempting, when regretting a previous decision, to avoid making another one, in case it proves to be another disaster. It's another way we can be stuck with the consequences. We read, though, that she has managed to put the geography right, at least. She has had the courage and wherewithal to return home and leave the past behind her, where it belongs. It's a positive move and most certainly one in the right direction, but it is not enough on its own. She travelled not with hope or optimism, but with despair and resignation. Perhaps she was only thinking ahead to where she wanted to be buried, once death had finally released her from her burdens.

What she did have, though (apart from God's unseen presence), was her sweet daughter-in-law, Ruth, in whom was embodied the sense that there was a future worth living for.

Sometimes, the consequences throw up delightful by-products. In my own life, a decision to move 150 miles east ultimately led to the breakdown of my marriage. How many times have I thought that, if only we hadn't moved, he wouldn't have met 'her'? Yet I cannot ignore the lovely fact that if we had stayed where we were, my son would not have met his wife. There is often a flip side.

With her precious Moabite daughter-in-law, we start to see a new role spring up for Naomi. The canvas of her life might have got over-painted with all kinds of horrors, but it will prove blank enough for God to paint a new story for her. I hope you can see, as I do, that there can be hope for us, too – even when we've learned to operate from a place of fatalism rather than faith.

Before God can rebuild us, there is often the need for dismantling first. Before Naomi could be restored, there needed to be some undoing of attitude, some challenge to what she'd learned to believe. There may have been a conclusion she had drawn that went along the lines of 'God wants me to stay empty'. She had been hungry in Bethlehem, and her pursuit of food had left her worse off than she could have imagined. Even with evidence of harvest all around her, she knew that she was only entitled to 'gleanings', the stalks dropped by the workers, left deliberately for the poor to gather. What must she have thought when Ruth returned with more grain than they could manage between them?

At the very least, it was a sign that God had a different perspective.

Despite things looking the way they did, there was some hope after all.

Perhaps better days were coming.

## Response

Regret is a natural reaction to a decision that's gone wrong, so this is not the place to squash those feelings down.

Be honest.

Tell God (using words if necessary) how you've been feeling. *God, I made such a bad choice... God, I wish I'd never... I want to curl up and hide... What a mess I've made of everything...*

Have you ever thought he might see it differently?

What if he was really saying something else? *Child, I loved that you were brave enough to take a risk... Child, you're still in my hands and my plan... Child, for this – and for every other thing – you have Jesus...*

What colour expresses how you feel now? Doodle with that colour as you yield yourself afresh to him today.

For further reflection and worship, listen to 'Greater than all my regrets' by Tenth Avenue North.

## Evening reflection: No going back

*We can never quite take back*
*or unsay what has been said.*
*We regret those words forever*
*that should have stayed within our head.*

*Ashamed, we try to back-track,*
*to attempt to justify,*
*but the damage is already done,*
*and we cannot explain why.*

*Nor can we ever untread a step,*
*each move made with full weight.*
*We see we've veered away, off-course,*
*only when it is too late.*

*We can try to make a U-turn*
*double-back on where we've come,*
*but we end up caught in circles*
*all-too-far away from home.*

*These and other choices*
*form the basis of regret:*
*the evidence of weakness*
*and the pride we'd best forget.*

*Thank God again for Jesus*
*who alone can make things right –*
*who can take the sting from what we've done*
*and point us to the light.*

# 10

# LEARNING FROM NAOMI: A HOPE-FILLED LEGACY

> **The women said to Naomi: 'Praise be to the Lord, who this day has not left you without a guardian-redeemer. May he become famous throughout Israel! He will renew your life and sustain you in your old age. For your daughter-in-law, who loves you and who is better to you than seven sons, has given him birth.'**
> RUTH 4:14–15

> **The widow who is really in need and left all alone puts her hope in God and continues night and day to pray and to ask God for help.**
> 1 TIMOTHY 5:5

The great thing about reading a story is that you get to see what everyone is up to. While Naomi is kept in the dark, you might say, we are privy to what her beloved daughter-in-law Ruth is up to – and it's quite a lot. Enter Boaz…

Ruth 2 introduces us to this relative of Naomi's late husband. With the implication that he is an older gentleman, we might suppose he would be a potential suitor for Naomi. Wouldn't that be sweet? The desolate widow returns to her roots, only to find fresh love waiting for her on her doorstep. But God's answers to prayer are often surprising and my Hollywood-esque version is not the one that plays out. Instead, we shall see that new hope – and reasons for living – arise in Naomi through the restoration of Ruth.

With Naomi's blessing, Ruth goes gleaning at the edges of the local barley fields, and it so happens that one of those fields belongs to Boaz, who just happens to visit his land to greet the harvesters. Astonishingly, with so many people around, his focus falls upon Ruth, who is working steadily, head bowed. Rather than one coincidence after another, though, we can take it as evidence that God is at work, orchestrating the tiny details that will make all the difference.

I want to highlight the comment Boaz makes to Ruth:

> **'I've been told all about what you have done for your mother-in-law since the death of your husband – how you left your father and mother and your homeland and came to live with a people you did not know before.'**
> RUTH 2:11

With our perspective so far being focused on Naomi, here is a glimpse of the other side of the story. Several thoughts were triggered as I read, not least how for years I struggled with the fifth commandment: 'Honour your father and your mother, so that you may live long in the land the Lord your God is giving you' (Exodus 20:12). I used to find my mother very difficult to get along with, and I often became frustrated with her. I lost count of the number of times I would pray to be able to honour her, to demonstrate my commitment to God by the way I spoke to her. Did Ruth need to pray along those lines, as she put up with Naomi's outbursts expressing her depression and despair? Did she have to bite her tongue as she heard – yet again – her complaints against God and the unfairness of life? I wouldn't be surprised if it were so.

Ruth's patient honouring of her mother-in-law not only soothed Naomi, but also brought blessing on herself through the good reputation it earned her. Faithfulness is a rewarder. If you are struggling to deal with someone difficult right now, please know that God sees and understands and wants to help. My prayer for you would echo that of Boaz for Ruth:

> **'May the Lord repay you for what you have done. May you be richly rewarded by the Lord, the God of Israel, under whose wings you have come to take refuge.'**
> RUTH 2:12

I've heard it said that Naomi was the typical Jewish mother: doing whatever she could for her family. I can certainly imagine the new twinkle in her eye, leaning in a bit more closely for news of her daughter-in-law's day.

'Wonderful grain today, dear. And so much of it.' Pauses to wipe the corner of her mouth. 'Where did you say you'd been working? And his name again?'

I imagine Naomi slapping her thigh in satisfaction at Ruth's mention of Boaz. But there was no time for resting on her laurels. Ruth would need a plan. And Naomi had already come up with one: stick with working in his fields, with his girls; after all, she needed to keep safe, didn't she?

It wasn't long before her true motivation was brought out into the open: Ruth couldn't live with her mother-in-law permanently; she needed a life of her own or, rather, a man she could share life with. Who better than Boaz, this 'guardian-redeemer', who had already led the charge in showing concern and kindness?

Naomi's scheme had no subtlety about it. She might as well have urged Ruth to put a sign round her neck, saying, 'Take me, I'm yours.' We can only imagine the surprise on Boaz's face when he wakes up in the middle of the night to find an attractive young woman lying at his feet! When Ruth returns home, laden with gifts of grain and his soft words running through her mind, Naomi is waiting, eager to find out whether her plan had worked.

It had.

A few practicalities dealt with, Boaz and Ruth are married and in due course have a son. Let's cut to the very end of the story. There is the most exquisite picture of Naomi cuddling her grandson – 'her son', as her friends put it. They're the women who have been the backdrop of her life, listening to her repeated tales of woe, commiserating over the hand she had been dealt. Their words, quoted at the start of today's reading, are a glorious summary of what God has done. She is now loved, not by a husband, but by a growing family. Her days (I imagine) of praying that her life might be shortened have been transformed. She has purpose, a reason to go on.

It's a beautiful end to the story, and its unusual plot is unlikely to mirror our own. But what it describes so eloquently is what God can do with lives that have lost their colour, their energy. When tragedy strikes repeatedly – as so often it can – it leaves us hollowed-out, emptied of hope. Naomi was blessed (some might even say lucky) that she had someone who was prepared to stick it out with her. It's not always the way these things go, with loneliness and isolation being the more frequent companions.

Is there anything wrong with trying to give God a hand, so to speak? It's an interesting question to answer. Why wouldn't we try to do something to make our situation better – unless we're so submerged by it that we're helpless to do anything? I guess the litmus test is whether we're acting out of faith or not. Are we pushing doors that we believe God has put before us, like Ruth gleaning in the right fields, or are we trying to kick our way in, thinking to ourselves that God is sitting back, doing nothing? Whether Naomi was guilty of manipulation is a matter of opinion, but I see a clear subtext (with all those little 'coincidences', for example) that God was the chief engineer. I like to think Naomi was simply his partner, working hand-in-hand, and that we could be, too.

What we absolutely have to remember is that God is able. Nothing is too hard for him. As I've already said, sometimes our prayers are answered in different ways than we imagine, but answer them he does; and he really does know best.

## Response

What parts of Naomi's story have resonated with you the most?

Is there one verse or detail that stands out?

Write it out – perhaps several times over – in as fancy lettering as you like. Let its truth sink in as you shape the words, knowing God is taking just as much care shaping the details of your life.

For further reflection and worship, listen to 'Restoration' by David Brymer.

## Evening reflection: Come, God of colour!

*'Spell it out in black and white,*
*what is it that you want?'*
*And the very question contained the answer,*
*much to our mutual surprise.*
*You see, the issue isn't really what I'm wanting,*
*but what is wanting in the issue:*
*colour,*
*vibrancy,*
*excitement (to push a point).*
*My life is so... so black and white,*
*so hollowed out,*
*that I'm a mere outline of myself.*
*Life in all its fullness*
*is what the Master promised,*
*while my mirror says different*
*and my heart agrees.*
*So, yes, I will spell out my prayer*
*in letters designed to be flooded with ink:*
*'Come, Holy Spirit,*
*bringer of life and all it entails.*
*Fill me with hope in the waiting,*
*patience in the receiving,*
*and gratitude for what's coming.*
*In God alone I put my trust,*
*this night and always.'*

# 11

# LEARNING FROM ELIJAH: THE POWER OF THE SPOKEN WORD

**Now Elijah the Tishbite, from Tishbe in Gilead, said to Ahab, 'As the Lord, the God of Israel, lives, whom I serve, there will be neither dew nor rain in the next few years except at my word.' Then the word of the Lord came to Elijah: 'Leave here, turn eastward and hide in the Kerith Ravine, east of the Jordan. You will drink from the brook, and I have instructed the ravens to supply you with food there.'**

1 KINGS 17:1–4

Over the next few days, we're going to delve into the story of the prophet Elijah, found in 1 Kings 17—19. He might have lived almost 2,900 years ago, but the issues he faced have a familiar ring about them, as we'll soon see.

First of all, some background context. Elijah lived in the northern kingdom of Israel at a troubled time in the nation's history. King Ahab is described as doing 'more evil in the eyes of the Lord than any of those before him' (1 Kings 16:30). That is quite a statement to make! He established the pagan religion of Baal to sit alongside the Jewish faith – 'Ahab also made an Asherah pole and did more to arouse the anger of the Lord, the God of Israel, than did all the kings of Israel before him' (1 Kings 16:33). His wife, Queen Jezebel, was a notoriously manipulative woman. Together, their rule was ruthless and merciless.

Enter Elijah.

If you have ever worked for a horrible boss or felt helpless in the face of bureaucracy, you will know how tight your throat gets even imagining standing up to them. But Elijah is a prophet, and it is his job to be confrontational. His statement is a cannonball shot across the bows of the monarchy: a drought is coming that will last several years.

Then God tells him to get out of there, fast.

This little detail is often overlooked, but I draw attention to it because some of us need to know how much God is looking out for us. He might call us into difficult situations and test us beyond what we would consider our natural limits, but he always has our back. What's more, Elijah wasn't even affected by the drought. God arranged for ravens to feed Elijah morning and night and then, when the water source dried up completely, he directed him to a place of shelter and sustenance.

Of course, a proper look at the biblical narrative corrects any impression of this being a five-star hotel. His landlady was in fact a poor widow, first mentioned gathering sticks for fuel. His request for water and bread seems presumptuous, considering she is preparing what will be the last meal for her and her son. The cupboards are bare. She is down to the crumbs.

Once more, Elijah speaks.

Have you ever had those moments when you realise too late you have said something out loud instead of keeping it in your head? I once bumped into someone I was dreading and actually said, 'Oh no, it's you.' In the context of Christian life, though, when I am aware of the Holy Spirit's anointing, I have been amazed again and again when I have heard myself say what I know I hadn't even been thinking. I see this little exchange between the widow and the prophet like that.

You see, if I were Elijah, my response would have been along the lines of: 'Oh, don't worry. Really sorry to have bothered you at such a tricky time. Hope it all works out…' Instead, having started with the nice touch of telling her not to worry, Elijah suggests that before she actions her plan for a Last Ever Supper, she should do a spot of baking for him. 'Serve me first,' he says, before adding – and I sense him standing a bit straighter here, looking her in the eye, with his voice coming more strongly – 'For this is what the Lord, the God of Israel, says: "The jar of flour will not be used up and the jug of oil will not run dry until the day the Lord sends rain on the land"' (1 Kings 17:14).

Let us pause for a moment, and activate our imagination.

Picture the scene I've described; allow yourself to be part of it. Are you a bystander, looking on, unable to believe your eyes and ears? Are you the son, powerless and dependent, waiting to see if his mother can turn things around? Or perhaps you can identify with this dear widow, already brought low, and now facing what she'd been dreading: no matter how careful she's been, she couldn't do enough. She is not enough.

This is raw weakness, isn't it? When we're at the end of ourselves and resigned to our fate. When other people around us are suffering, too, so there's nowhere else to turn.

What effect does Elijah's prophecy have on the woman, as you imagine it?

In other places in the Bible, when God says something ridiculous, like, 'I know you're incredibly old and went through the menopause donkeys years ago, but next year you'll have a baby' (this happened to Abraham's wife Sarah, see Genesis 18:9–15 and 21:1–7), the person laughs or bats it away. What does the widow do? She goes straight home and follows his instructions. They eat well that night, no room for seconds, and again the next day, and the next. The level on the flour container and the oil jug doesn't budge, no matter how much she uses. Elijah's words have heralded a miracle.

It is wise to point out that it wasn't an automatic 'happy ever after', despite the incredible everlasting food. The story goes on to tell us that this woman's son, the one spared from starvation and destitution, succumbed to a horrible illness and died. The bereaved mother is angry, and lets rip at Elijah. She connects this event with her own sin and immediately views the man of God as wishing her harm after all.

There are several things on the line here: the life of the son, the happiness of the mother, the reputation of Elijah, and the honour of God. In praying, desperately, 'Lord my God, have you brought tragedy even on this widow I am staying with, by causing her son to die?' (1 Kings 17:20), I see Elijah having no concern for himself. Without any knowledge of CPR, Elijah relies on God's instructions and sees the boy come back to life. Yet another miracle, praise God!

Let us linger for a moment on what the relieved mother says: 'Now I know that you are a man of God and that the word of the Lord from your mouth is the truth' (1 Kings 17:24). She has already experienced day after day of supernatural provision, proving that what Elijah promised her was true. But it is possible she didn't even see God in it. It is possible that we miss him, too. it took the resurrection of her son to get her to truly believe. What will it take for us?

You see, we need to know that God sees us when we are at our weakest, and he wants to help. That help will take many different forms, but often it comes through a verse of scripture, a direct word of prophecy, or something a Christian friend says. Sometimes those promises take a long time to be fulfilled and we can grow despairing of whether that thing will ever happen. The question is whether we can truly believe, even while we're still waiting.

God is still concerned for each situation that brings us grief and loss. He is, too, concerned for his reputation. He wants us to take him at his word and then rejoice when it comes to be.

He wants that for each of us, today.

## Response

Today's message came in the form of a story.

Have you ever tried writing down what has happened to you as if it's a short story (featuring someone else perhaps)?

You don't have to worry about how well it's written (no one else needs to see it), but let your imagination fly.

How does the story end? How would you like it to end?

If God is one of the characters, what do you hear him say and watch him do?

For further reflection and worship, listen to 'Your words' by Third Day.

## Evening reflection: What words can do

*The power of words*
*to build up or tear down,*
*encourage a soul or cause them sorrow,*
*to reveal truth or continue a lie –*
*the choice is ours, daily.*
*Do we listen to what God says,*
*pay close enough attention*
*that we could repeat it, verbatim,*
*if we had to?*
*Or do we grab the gist,*
*clutch at key words,*
*and miss the moment of miracle?*
*Let me be one, O Lord,*
*who follows so closely*
*that I hear your heartbeat*
*as well as your words.*
*Let me put them into practice,*
*convert them into action,*
*so the living word once more has flesh*
*that can touch the needy.*
*Let me not question what you say*
*or doubt its meaning.*
*Let me only obey*
*and watch what you will do.*

# 12
# LEARNING FROM ELIJAH: STILL STANDING

**For our struggle is not against flesh and blood, but against the rulers, against the authorities, against the powers of this dark world and against the spiritual forces of evil in the heavenly realms. Therefore put on the full armour of God, so that when the day of evil comes, you may be able to stand your ground, and after you have done everything, to stand.**
EPHESIANS 6:12–13

**The prayer of a righteous person is powerful and effective. Elijah was a human being, even as we are. He prayed earnestly that it would not rain, and it did not rain on the land for three and a half years. Again he prayed, and the heavens gave rain, and the earth produced its crops.**
JAMES 5:16–18

The plotline of today's continuing story of Elijah is filled with suspense, adventure, and mountain-top exhilaration. It's year three of the nationwide drought, with failed crops, uncertainty, and discomfort, topped off by a reckless and unpredictable king and queen. It is easy to imagine the grinding hopelessness and fear felt by their citizens.

Thank God for people of courage like Elijah, who are prepared to make a stand.

Challenged by fellow prophet Obadiah, Elijah returns to King Ahab and demands a face-off, the entire population invited to watch. They will witness definitive proof that Yahweh, the God of Israel, is supreme and that Baal is nothing. Let the 450 prophets of Baal be pitted against the one prophet of Yahweh and see what happens.

If you've ever had to do a Very Brave Thing, you'll know how fine a line it is between courage and folly. What must it have looked like from the perspective of the 450 prophets of Baal, plus 400 prophets of Asherah, plus however many of the nation's inhabitants that came long? It was bad enough when the shepherd boy David stood up to Goliath, but this?

Are you sure, Elijah? Has God really said…?

Elijah has already shown incredible boldness in predicting the famine to a hostile monarch; now he is rebuking the king in no uncertain terms:

> **'I have not made trouble for Israel,' Elijah replied. 'But you and your father's family have. You have abandoned the Lord's commands and have followed the Baals.'**
> 1 KINGS 18:18

Do you imagine his voice clear and bold? Or notice the slight tremor and the clearing of his throat? Sometimes, standing up for God can feel terrifying on the inside.

Mount Carmel, meaning 'vineyard' or 'garden', was a wooded mountain ridge, where Ahab had constructed an altar to Baal. Here, in full sight, Elijah issued the stark choice the Israelites faced:

> **'How long will you waver between two opinions? If the Lord is God, follow him; but if Baal is God, follow him.'**
> 1 KINGS 18:21

The people are told to bring two bulls up to the mountain, one for each side. Team Baal went first, preparing their bull for sacrifice and calling on their god to light the fire. From morning until night, they shouted, danced, and shouted some more. Increasingly desperate, they got swords and spears and cut themselves, as if they were the sacrifice, after all.

The result: a big, fat nothing.

Now, before we go on to the rest of the story – and it's a great one – I want to point something out. We never need to go to these kinds of lengths to get God to notice us! Don't get me wrong, I have been there. I have done the shouting and hollering and the rephrasing of prayers, in case my words weren't up to par. I have got up at 5.00 am to pray. I have fasted. I have made bargains. Desperation will make us do that. But, believe me, there is not a moment we don't have God's attention (Psalm 139:2–3).

Here's the thing, though: the reason why the efforts of those prophets didn't work is really simple – their 'god' didn't exist.

Here's the other – really great – thing: ours does.

Let's read on.

What happens next is an extraordinary display of strength from Elijah. His physical outlay is colossal. He had no team to draw on. When he is described as preparing the bull and rebuilding the altar, it is by his handiwork alone. He takes twelve (substantial) stones to represent each tribe, and builds an altar (an altar, note, that is big enough to hold a dissected bull). He digs a trench around it, again single-handed, before butchering the dead animal and heaving it into place. Only then does he call for some help: to fill the twelve large jars of water and have them poured over what he has built.

This is just the preparation.

Isn't it extraordinary what a person can achieve when they sense God inspiring them?

Each step was a superhuman one, stretching him beyond the limits of physical capacity. We can only imagine his exhaustion. But there was more stretching to come.

It was time for God to show up.

In far less taxing circumstances, I have been conscious of my unbidden prayer: 'God, if you don't show up here, I'm stuck.' Those times when we have stepped out of our comfort zone and feel we have no back-up. When we have perhaps made a bold declaration of some sort, and we will look a right chump if nothing happens. When we have prayed, and there's that horrible aching silence while we wait for an answer.

We just noted that the prophets of Baal were so ineffective in their praying because they were appealing to a false god, even one known as the god of rain and storm, among other things. Well, let's turn that right around: the reason Elijah was so confident was because he knew the absolute, unshaking reality of his God. Why else would he make it so difficult? Numerically, he was totally on the back foot. Politically, he was exposed in a way that the king's cronies never would be. Scientifically, he makes things as hard as they could possibly be, by soaking everything with water drawn from the natural spring which defied the ongoing drought.

Elijah's prayer simply stated:

> **'Lord, the God of Abraham, Isaac and Israel, let it be known today that you are God in Israel and that I am your servant and have done all these things at your command. Answer me, Lord, answer me, so these people will know that you, Lord, are God, and that you are turning their hearts back again.'**
>
> 1 KINGS 18:36–37

Only the repeated 'Answer me' betrays his urgency (I would have been adding, 'please, please, please' under my breath).

It was enough.

God came through with not so much as a hesitation.

The answer was definitive and unequivocal.

'The Lord – he is God!' (1 Kings 18:39) was the response of the Israelites, while the hapless prophets were chased into the valley below, where they met their death.

As for Elijah, he climbed back to the top of Mount Carmel and spent a moment in quiet reflection, bent double, head between his knees. Exhausted, but no doubt utterly grateful and relieved it was over. Taking a deep breath, he stretched himself to standing as he sensed God's fresh anointing.

Rain was coming!

Hitching up his robes and setting his face to the horizon, he outran Ahab's chariot the considerable distance to Jezreel as the storm broke.

God was still on the move!

## Response

Elijah is portrayed here as phenomenally strong: physically, spiritually, and in resolve and resilience.

Where do you think that strength came from?

Are there any aspects of the story that you can relate to in your life at the moment – and seek God's strength in?

*God, you are real and mighty and awesome. Thank you for Elijah's story of trust and courage. I don't feel brave very often, and I'm all too aware of my weakness. Come through for me, God, please! Let me be still standing, still faithful, still holding on when the storms come, I pray. Amen.*

For further reflection and worship, listen to 'You're still God' by Philippa Hanna.

## Evening reflection: Our daily battle

*Daily are the battles,*
*constant is the fight.*
*Ever looming over me*
*the need to choose what's right.*

*In facing opposition*
*I am tempted just to cave,*
*to let them do what they will do,*
*I'm sick of being brave.*

*Yet voices carry on the wind*
*the truths that bring relief:*
*he's God, he's good, he's always there:*
*therein my source of peace.*

*It's true I have to play my part,*
*according to his call;*
*but with his strength, I know I'll stand*
*while those against me fall.*

# 13

# LEARNING FROM ELIJAH: WHEN WE'RE AT THE END OF OUR TETHER

**Elijah was afraid and ran for his life. When he came to Beersheba in Judah, he left his servant there, while he himself went a day's journey into the wilderness. He came to a broom bush, sat down under it and prayed that he might die. 'I have had enough, Lord,' he said. 'Take my life; I am no better than my ancestors.' Then he lay down under the bush and fell asleep.**
1 KINGS 19:3–5

**The Lord is trustworthy in all he promises and faithful in all he does. The Lord upholds all who fall and lifts up all who are bowed down. The eyes of all look to you, and you give them their food at the proper time.**
PSALM 145:13–15

If I ask a friend how they are and they answer, 'Tired', I usually follow it up with, 'Tired from something nice or something nasty?' Feeling tired after a fantastic trip is worth suffering afterwards for. Feeling tired because you're worn down by everything life demands of you is an entirely different matter.

We are back with Elijah today, and this passage in 1 Kings 19 is one of my favourites. I recommend reading through the whole chapter now, and leaving the Bible open as we go through. Anyone who struggles to connect with the God of the Old Testament might find a surprising (but so lovely) demonstration of how kind and tender and compassionate God really is.

Elijah is tired. No wonder.

Physically, the Mount Carmel episode would have stretched the most robust, gym-bodied person. He had built an altar, hefting great stones around, then butchered a bull. He had chased 450 men down into the valley, then climbed back up to the mountaintop to seek God. At the sight of a promise-laden cloud, he set off to run another set of kilometres, beating the king in his chariot to Jezreel.

Spiritually, Elijah sought God again and again, straining to hear the voice that would guide him. Obedient, he acted on what God said, apparently unconcerned for his personal welfare.

Mentally and emotionally, he'd had to stand up to the country's tyrannical rulers, no doubt acting braver than he felt and biting down his fears.

None of this is to say he did it without God's power or anointing. Frankly, he would have collapsed long before now if he was relying on his own strength. But any of us who have 'stepped out for God' in any capacity will know that eventually we reach our limit.

'I'm at the end of my tether,' we might whisper into the night.

God hears, and knows, and understands, and – wonderfully – is holding the other end of that tether and won't, *can't*, let go.

Pause a moment, perhaps imagining yourself holding that rope, with Jesus so near…

So, news reaches Elijah that the queen is out to kill him. It's the final straw. He must have hoped that the triumph of Yahweh over Baal would be the last word on the subject. Instead, he finds himself running once more, for his life this time, and ends up collapsed under a broom tree. It is not huge, not much bigger than a man's height, but shelter is shelter when you're in the desert. He falls asleep. He's done in.

It's shocking just how quickly the encroaching tide of despair can come in. As someone who has known mental breakdown, I know how thin the line can be between feeling okay and not, between coping and going under. While I was suffering from depression, another car rear-ended mine as I was stationary. It was enough to give me whiplash, as well as writing off my poor car, and I was persuaded to go for compensation. At the medical interview, the doctor repeatedly asked me, 'But why are you depressed?' I told him more of the story (it ran to several chapters) and again he asked, 'But why are you depressed?' I felt frustrated I couldn't make him understand, despite my careful explanation. The only conclusion I could draw was that he had no empathy. What wonderful relief there is in knowing God is not like that!

> **For we do not have a high priest who is unable to feel sympathy for our weaknesses, but we have one who has been tempted in every way, just as we are – yet he did not sin.**
> HEBREWS 4:15

Let's read on and see how it plays out with Elijah.

Elijah has barely fallen asleep when an angel disturbs him, urging him to eat. It must have felt like a dream, though the freshly baked bread and jug of cool water were no illusion. His belly full, he fell back into the oblivion of sleep, only for the episode to be repeated.

It's a curious corner of the story. It brings to the fore the question of how we think God views us when we are in crisis. If we're honest, we probably base our thinking on how other people have treated us, kind of assuming that God will be the same. I remember clearly the morning my pastor's wife phoned me to find out if I was planning to come along to the prayer meeting. I told her no, that I had a kidney infection and was going nowhere. Her reply? 'Don't you know you're more than a conqueror?'

If ever you have had scripture aimed at you like a weapon, I want to assure you that God does not speak to us like that! His words bring life and wholeness, peace and reassurance.

See how gently God deals with Elijah here. He had something to say to him, but that could wait. Elijah was empty. He needed sleep and simple food, administered with tenderness, before he could face anything else.

Fortified, Elijah journeys on, 40 days and nights through the desert, to reach another mountain. Also known as Mount Sinai, Horeb is the place where God gave the ten commandments to Moses. Did Elijah need to go back to the roots of his faith, to seek the one behind it all? Was he aiming for a kind of factory reset? God is there, waiting, and asks Elijah what he is doing there. I hear no rebuke in God's tone. Nor do I hear ignorance of Elijah's state. Instead, I think this is an invitation for Elijah to express it in his own words, and it is a succinct summary: 'I'm the only one who cares for your ways, God! I've got into this mess because of you!'

God responds with a display of his power – through wind, earthquake, and fire – that isn't intended, in my opinion, to shut Elijah down but to ground him. He is almighty, ruler of the elements – and Elijah's Lord. Then, with a whisper that may have been Elijah's name, but in any case had him leaning in to catch what was said, God settles the matter. I believe he wants to do the same for us today.

We are never on our own, though we may feel like we are.

God has great plans for what happens next and will be with us when we get up from his presence in a moment.

Help is coming.

Hold on tight.

## Response

If Elijah's story has resonated with you today, then the response I suggest is not one of action but of rest.

If you identify with being at the end of your tether, then there is absolutely no shame in admitting it: to yourself and to God. He waits to hear you say it, and he has nothing but compassion for you.

Can you take some time off today? Or schedule some in, very soon?

Can you go for a walk or visit that special place where you always feel better?

Can you treat yourself to a 'little something'?

God wants to take care of you. It would be a really good idea to let him.

Be blessed as you do.

For further reflection and worship, listen to 'God help me' by Unspoken.

## Evening reflection: Earth, wind, fire, and whisper

*Shaken by earthquake*
*I know that feeling well*
*of being knocked off my feet,*
*uprooted from connection.*
*It's what a day will do sometimes.*

*Winds of change, their roaring fury*
*flattening my best-laid plans*
*and making foolish all my wisdom.*
*Demolished hope now rubble.*
*How can God be in this?*

*Burned by fire, there's that, too,*
*when words hissed out*
*in the heat of the moment*
*make wastelands of friendship.*
*Come, Lord Jesus!*

*A whisper that I'd miss by day*
*but with life's volume turned to low*
*at night I catch it in the air:*
*my name in hush, in breath.*
*Listen…*
*Take note…*

*This the sound that stills my soul*
*calling me to lean in closer,*
*ears straining, heart yearning*
*to hear its repeat.*
*Can you hear it, too?*

# 14

# WHEN WE FEEL LONELY AND ISOLATED

**He replied, 'I have been very zealous for the Lord God Almighty. The Israelites have rejected your covenant, torn down your altars, and put your prophets to death with the sword. I am the only one left, and now they are trying to kill me too.'**
1 KINGS 19:10

**And let us consider how we may spur one another on towards love and good deeds, not giving up meeting together, as some are in the habit of doing, but encouraging one another – and all the more as you see the Day approaching.**
HEBREWS 10:24–25

In all our daily explorations, my priority is to reflect God's perspective on the issues. But when it comes to talking about isolation, it feels like swimming against a powerful cultural current. Our society values independence, we have always known that, but there has been a powerful escalation in recent years. A Google search of 'positive quotes about being alone' uncovered these examples:

- 'Pretending to be happy when you're alone is an example of how strong you are as a person.'
- 'If you want to be strong, learn how to enjoy being alone.'
- 'Standing alone doesn't mean I am alone. It means I'm strong enough to handle all things by myself.'

These quotes, and the many others I could have included, are positively prizing the notion that 'I have no need of anyone else at all. I am enough.'

Weak? Me? Because I'm alone? Get out of here!

Needless to say, this isn't the line I am taking today. We need God in our lives: we absolutely do. We cannot do a minute of it without him – nor were we ever intended to. It is nothing to do with how capable we are, nor what a successful life we are enjoying as an introvert, nor how much we enjoy our own company. We need others around us.

Some of us may be genuinely enjoying a season or entire lifetime of aloneness. I have had the privilege of this in the past, living with Jesus as my companion and experiencing his presence in outstanding ways. Along with the apostle Paul, I could attest to the benefits of being able to focus on God. To be clear, there were real downsides too (not least, having to do everything myself), but the season was a positive one, overall.

Some of us, though, may be desperately lonely, for which I have deep empathy. Needing company and support, everyone else seems too busy, perhaps too tied up with their glorious 'I am enough!' living to even notice us. In this kind of season, we may have concluded that we're not enough. Aloneness is not a joy, but a burden. 'One' is certainly not 'fun'.

Then there are others of us who have become isolated through circumstances. Perhaps it is because of being a carer or being unwell/disabled ourselves, not easily able to leave the house, if at all. Perhaps there is no convenient access to transport. Or perhaps we are living in a house full of other people but feel so misunderstood and unaccepted that we might as well be alone.

Whatever our situation, we must lay aside the horrible mottoes of those motivational quotes. They are not expressing strength, but only pride and bravado. The truth is that long-term isolation is not good for us; in fact, it weakens and hurts us. I think God has something to say to us about all that.

If you have ever heard the phrase 'divide and conquer', you will know that it is an effective way of controlling people and manipulating events. I believe that Satan uses this strategy against God's people. When we are enjoying healthy fellowship with each other and valuing our togetherness, we are a formidable force for good. Love lies at the heart of our unity, and unity is also the best method of demonstrating that love to those around us. What better way is there of rendering our witness powerless than driving wedges between people? That wedge might be suspicion, jealousy, or rivalry, all of which serve to separate us from each other, diluting our impact and cutting at the heart of being church.

Sadly, we all learn the pain of separation and its resulting isolation at an early age. Nursery-age children are snubbed by 'friends' who don't want to play with them anymore. Siblings become competitive instead of remembering they are on the family team. And so it goes on. Some of us have endured so much pain from relationships that we cannot face another one. There is a reason why people choose to live with cats. Or dogs.

Today's scripture passages highlight two contrasting areas of focus. In the first, Elijah (as we've seen) was at his lowest ebb and is in conversation with God at Mount Horeb. Asked, 'Why are you here, Elijah?' the prophet pours out his woes, including the 'fact' that he was the only God-fearing man left in Israel. How quickly we can feel alone, and how sapping is that belief. I believe it is one of the enemy's most common lies. In the British Post Office scandal, dramatised in the 2024, TV series *Mr Bates vs The Post Office*, every one of the subpostmasters was told that they were the only one reporting the problem with the Horizon software. In that instance, there proved to be many hundreds affected. In Elijah's case, there were 7,000 other believers still alive and well.

The second passage reminds us how easy it is to lose the habit of togetherness. One Sunday is missed because there is something we need to do, but the next week there is something else. Before we even realise what has happened, our church-going has been replaced by other things, our church friends by other people. You see, even within the church we are not immune to the 'me-me-me' culture all around us. We might defend our choices by saying that it is our vertical relationship – us and Jesus – that is the priority, and that the horizontal ones with our fellow believers are an indulgence we can do without. But the Bible never agrees. Our need for each other is integral to our Christian life. Without the encouragement and challenge and provocation of others – to say nothing of the joy of spending time with others who love Jesus – our lives are the poorer. And, I'm sorry to say, we make it far easier for our enemy to pick us off when we are not tightly knitted into the pack.

There is one more aspect of isolation to remember. As we have already seen, in the garden of Eden it was the shame arising from their sin that made Adam and Eve want to cover up and hide. They found it was their first instinct once they had disobeyed God by eating the fruit from the forbidden tree; and it is an instinct we have all inherited. As easily as throwing on a comfy jumper, we slap a mask on to try to cover up in front of other people and, knowing we can't hide before God, we avoid him altogether.

Sin is such a separator. Let's all make sure, please, that there is nothing in our lives that is keeping us away from other people.

## Response

Some of what we have read today may have touched a nerve, and it is important we don't miss the chance to put things right.

As ever, honesty is key: both with ourselves and with God.

Are there areas of your life you feel alone in?

How is that affecting you?

Are there people you have been pushing away?

Can you be honest about why that is so?

Is there someone you can reach out to this week?

*God, thank you for your constant presence, made available through the Holy Spirit. Thank you that you have not left us as orphans, nor will you ever leave us or forsake us. Forgive us for the ways we have spoiled our relationships, and the reactions we have made to that pain. Heal us and help us, Lord. We want to do life your way, for your glory. Amen.*

For further reflection and worship, listen to 'I am not alone' by Kari Jobe.

## Evening reflection: Alone no more

*I'm all alone,*
*just as I feared;*
*misunderstood, misrepresented,*
*no ally or friend to speak of.*
*I've read the signs,*
*the mottoes on mugs,*
*that tell me I'm strong and capable*
*just as I am,*
*no need for others*
*to mess up my home or my time or my heart.*
*But to listen to that*
*is to make me the mug,*
*isn't it?*
*Instead, I turn to God,*
*who always speaks a better word.*
*It is not good for us to be alone.*
*I will send another counsellor.*
*I will never leave you nor forsake you.*
*He sets the lonely in families.*
*These are the truths I will cling to*
*and not the flimsy raft of experience.*
*Show me, God, who I can be a good friend to,*
*a good sister or brother,*
*a good team-mate.*
*I think I'd like to try your way of doing things,*
*if that's alright.*

# 15
# WHEN WE ARE ILL

**As he went along, he saw a man blind from birth. His disciples asked him, 'Rabbi, who sinned, this man or his parents, that he was born blind?' 'Neither this man nor his parents sinned,' said Jesus, 'but this happened so that the works of God might be displayed in him.'**
JOHN 9:1–3

**When Jesus landed and saw a large crowd, he had compassion on them and healed those who were ill.**
MATTHEW 14:14

Even the healthiest of us get ill sooner or later, whether that's physically, mentally, or emotionally. It's horrible being ill. At best it makes us feel grotty, but at its worst it has far-reaching repercussions, affecting the lives of everyone around us. We can find ourselves worried about symptoms and scrabbling for answers to questions we hardly dare voice.

When will I feel better? Is this 'it'?

If it is, what's going to happen to me and my family?

What have I done to deserve this?

What use am I to anyone, let alone God, when I'm so weak right now?

What happened to the promise of 'life in all its fullness'?

We may be praying for healing, knowing that when Jesus walked the earth he had compassion on the sick, who came in vast numbers.

That subject, though, is beyond the scope of this chapter, and there are many other helpful books available on the topic. Instead, I want us to focus on the real answer to our questions: God himself. This is no glib statement. No attempt to sidestep the issue. Not just in the area of healing, but in all things, we seek God for who he is, not just what he can do for us.

Our view of God is always affected by what we are going through. When life is going well, we can sing 'God is good' and mean it from the depths of our hearts. In a harder context, the same words can get stuck in our throats.

God is good – life is good – I know it to be true.

God is good – but life is so hard – is God good?

God is good? – Really? – I'm not so sure…

I want to say, emphatically, that God is good, all the time. And, perhaps more crucially, that when we have got that absolutely clear, then it makes the bad times more bearable. Jesus said:

> **'Which of you, if your son asks for bread, will give him a stone? Or if he asks for a fish, will give him a snake? If you, then, though you are evil, know how to give good gifts to your children, how much more will your Father in heaven give good gifts to those who ask him!'**
>
> MATTHEW 7:9–11

God doesn't answer our requests for his goodness by giving out mean things. He doesn't send sickness to punish us in some way. In the Old Testament we can read the story of Job, a devout believer who met with terrible suffering. His friends tried to help, but their bottom line was the established belief at the time: if you're suffering, you must have sinned. Such were the words of Eliphaz:

> **'Consider now: who, being innocent, has ever perished? Where were the upright ever destroyed? As I have observed, those who plough evil and those who sow trouble reap it.'**
> JOB 4:7–8

Perhaps someone has told you that, too. Or maybe a little voice in your head.

'You reap what you sow.'

'It's your fault.'

'It's because you…'

I can't refute that more strongly. It's simply not the truth.

The best way I can illustrate this is through the story of someone who knows. I had the joy and privilege of interviewing Lydia, who loves Jesus deeply and has recently returned to work after completing her treatment for breast cancer. She admitted there had been many tears along the way, but what shone through as we spoke was how her belief in the goodness of God had proved true, again and again. When her mother had died of cancer, when Lydia was only a teenager, God had amazingly 'rose-colour-washed' what should have been the worst of all summers. She had ended up having fun times and adventures with friends and, amazingly, could now look on that as the best summer of her childhood. She held on to the real expectation that God could do it again in her cancer journey. And he did.

She spoke of the special blessing of having time to delve into the Bible, exploring the wilderness experiences of others. And God dealt with her specific fears that, throughout her debilitating chemo treatment, she wouldn't be well enough to greet her son from high school and cook his dinner. She described what a gift of grace it had been to find that, on the vast majority of days, she was able to be 'up like magic at 4.00 pm' and meet his needs, before returning to resting.

I couldn't help but probe deeper: surely what she was describing was not typical? What was she drawing on that made her able to respond to cancer like that? Her answer was softly spoken: 'It's the love of God. I just love him… I just trust him.' Was she ever tempted to think this was some kind of punishment or to doubt that God is good? 'No. We live in a rotten world and we get caught in the cross-fire, don't we?'

When I asked whether her suffering had affected her connection with God, she replied only that it was 'more of him being wonderful'. She believes strongly that loving and trusting God in the good times is what prepares us for doing so when life is tough. Resting in God, she said, is the only place we find real rest, and hope, too.

Those of us that wonder if we could ever talk of illness in those ways might be encouraged by what Lydia went on to say. She laughed in talking of the Weebles toys (developed in 1971 by Playskool), that were weighted in the bottom so they could wobble, sometimes violently, from side to side but always bobbed upright again. Their advertising jingle was: 'Weebles wobble but they don't fall down!' 'It doesn't matter if we fall down,' Lydia said. 'I don't know what will happen in the future, but I don't worry about not being able to stay upright, because at those times we have our Christian family to come alongside and lift us and carry us. Jesus doesn't mind if we can't stand up… When you go through things like this, we will wobble, wobble all over the place, but I don't think the Lord minds.'

None of us would volunteer to suffer through ill health, and yet it's the path we are often called to walk down. It's one marked with weakness, fear, uncertainty, and doubt, but our good, good God walks with us and carries us. Lydia modelled so powerfully the truth the apostle Paul shared from his own suffering:

> **But he said to me, 'My grace is sufficient for you, for my power is made perfect in weakness.' Therefore I will boast all the more gladly about my weaknesses, so that Christ's power may rest on me.**
> 2 CORINTHIANS 12:9

How can such an upside-down message be true?

Only because God is good.

## Response

There are several images to draw from today.

Do you feel like a 'feeble Weeble', quivering and shaking? It's perfectly okay to tell God about it, and ask him to hold you steady.

Have you been wondering if God is really good? Ask him to remind you of a time you were more sure, and thank him for it.

If you're simply feeling rotten, Jesus is reaching out to you in compassion. Can you feel it?

*God of all kindness, of mercy and grace, come near, we pray. We need your touch, your help. Take our fears and doubts and weave your love in and through all we're going through. For our sake and for your glory, Amen.*

For further reflection and worship, listen to 'God, you're so good' by Passion and Kristian Stanfill.

## Evening reflection: Embraced by mercy

*Lord, have mercy, in this evening hour;*
*Christ, have mercy, on the one you love;*
*Lord, have mercy, I pray from a full heart.*
*My body is weak, you know it, Lord,*
*and I lean into your embrace,*
*relieved at another day done.*
*I'm not always brave*
*in the face of trouble,*
*nor filled with faith*
*in the times of pain,*
*yet I come.*
*I always need to come.*
*Like a child I clamber on to your lap,*
*dishevelled and weary.*
*Your arms catching me, holding me tight.*
*Here, here, is where I need to stay,*
*listening to your heartbeat*
*settling my own.*
*My questions can wait a while.*
*What matters can matter later.*
*All is well with my soul.*

# 16

# WHEN SIN CAUSES TROUBLE

**Have mercy on me, O God, according to your unfailing love; according to your great compassion blot out my transgressions. Wash away all my iniquity and cleanse me from my sin. For I know my transgressions, and my sin is always before me.**
PSALM 51:1–3

We uncovered the issue of consequences in Naomi's story. Every decision we take or don't take – every action or inaction – causes something else to happen, either to ourselves and our circumstances or to others and theirs. Just think about the set of ripples produced when a stone is dropped into a pond. Even when you're dropping it really, really carefully, the water betrays what you've done. It always shows.

We're looking today at the ways in which sin weakens us. Put better, how sin *and its consequences* weaken us. Some of us are in difficulty because of our mistakes or our deliberate actions, and some of us are enduring lasting pain from having been sinned against. Since the disastrous 'apple' moment in the garden of Eden, all of us *without exception* have been living with sin as our constant enemy and our frequent tempter. However, vitally importantly, ever since that seminal moment on the cross, all of us *without exception* have free and full access to transformational forgiveness issued by God himself.

**For all have sinned and fall short of the glory of God, and all are justified freely by his grace through the redemption that came by Christ Jesus.**
ROMANS 3:23–24

Read those verses again. Without this truth as our backdrop, we will remain stuck and fail to see the hope for both the sinner and the sinned-against.

Let's consider the 'sinner' first, through the story of King David (as narrated in 1 Samuel 16—31, 2 Samuel, and 1 Kings 1—2). When God chose him to become king of Israel, he was nothing but a shepherd boy, albeit one who had developed good character as he worked with the sheep and dealt with his patronising brothers. 'The Lord has sought out a man after his own heart and appointed him ruler of his people' (1 Samuel 13:14). What a description! What an endorsement!

Perhaps we started well, too.

Despite David being anointed king, Saul was still on the throne, making life incredibly difficult for David. Nevertheless, the young lad was the one chosen to soothe Saul's rages, playing Spirit-inspired music and bringing peace which transcends understanding.

Perhaps we once moved in God's anointing, too.

Eventually, Saul died and David entered fully into his God-ordained destiny. His life was blessed and honoured by God and the whole nation benefitted. But then.

This next chapter of David's life runs counter to everything described so far. How adultery and murder could be committed by a man so highly favoured, of such godly character, might seem a mystery. It only proves that *any of us are capable of anything*.

Perhaps we've been surprised by our own sin, too.

Some of us, like David, have been in the wrong place at the wrong time (David should have been in battle, alongside his fighting men; see 2 Samuel 11:1). We have been tempted to look, then fallen into sin by a second look, followed by acting on what we saw. This is how 'innocently' it can all start, but God never views it lightly, and nor should we.

David's sin had powerful consequences. The baby conceived through adultery died, and violence became a hallmark of David's family. But the most powerful consequence of all was David's response to his failing and his subsequent restoration.

I can easily think of people who have blundered through life, actively sinful and astonishingly lacking in self-awareness. If God has pricked their conscience, they've soon got over it. They are destined, it seems, to perpetuate their poor behaviour their whole life long.

Not so with David.

The 'man after God's own heart' was still in there, somewhere, and when God brought him to the point of repentance (2 Samuel 12:7), there is no doubt it was genuine and life-changing.

We cannot get our heads around how it works, how God can take away our shame and sin's intolerable burden, even transforming the consequences. This is all part of God's grace and mercy, treating us differently from what we deserve. While the enemy would constantly remind us of what we have done, the arms of Jesus are ever extended, as they were on the cross, with the invitation to come near and sort things out (Isaiah 1:18).

David came before God in heart-felt, soul-wrenching sorrow and repented, expressing it in ways we can echo, in Psalm 51.

Perhaps we should repent, too.

When it comes to being sinned against, it's a different dynamic, but the principles are the same. Being the victim of sin or even crime inevitably weakens us, but sin should never have the final word. The consequences are dire and often involve tragic degrees of loss, but God never wants us to be stuck underneath the terrible burden of what someone else has done against us.

Our reaction might be to harden our hearts, to vow that 'no one will treat us like that again', and to plan revenge. Gently I have to say – as one who has been there, believe me – this is not the way. Offering forgiveness is never about saying 'It's okay'. What happened to you is absolutely not okay. But when we don't forgive, we bear a weight we were not designed to carry. This is not about letting the perpetrator off the hook, but of us being set free.

Forgiving someone else is for our benefit. (Leave it up to God to sort them out…)

When I was badly sinned against, I knew I had to forgive them but I simply couldn't. It was too raw and too soon. But I pledged to God that I did want to eventually. It took over a year, and I didn't feel any more like doing it when I actually did, but when I prayed, 'Lord, I forgive ________________________ from my heart,' I can't describe the feeling of God's blessings rushing in! I was still living with the consequences of what had been done to me, but the weight of it had gone. It was a miracle, truly.

Sin makes us 'less than' by distorting God's image in us, separating us from God, spoiling our relationships, and keeping us ashamed.

God's forgiveness makes us 'more than' by renewing our connection with him, displaying God's love for all to see, and restoring our God-given glory.

We do not have to stay weakened within sin's grip.

We can be set free.

## Response

There's nothing to be afraid of. Our sin separates us from God, but Jesus is always, always, the bridge by which we regain access.

**For repentance:**

If you can, put your hands into something mucky: some soil or something sticky. Ask for the Holy Spirit to come as you admit to God the sin you have done. Don't resist the feelings of shame – they are necessary to the process – but give them to him along with your confession. Use David's words in Psalm 51 if they help.

As you wash your hands, watching your 'sin' swirl down the plughole, receive his forgiveness and offer your thanks.

**For offering forgiveness:**

Remember, you may not feel like doing this, but you can still make the decision.

Asking for the Holy Spirit to come, say out loud who has hurt you and what they have done. Speak out your forgiveness, using these words if they help:

*God, I name ______________________ as the one who has hurt me by ___________________________. In Jesus' name I choose to forgive them for every way they have hurt and harmed me. I no longer hold them to account but leave them in your hands, to deal with as you choose. I trust you to complete what you have started. Amen.*

For further reflection and worship, listen to 'O come to the altar' by Elevation Worship.

## Evening reflection: The pointing finger

*'It was them!'*
*Cheeks grow hot at the accusations*
*intended to deflect the guilt*
*away from me,*
*yes, far away, please.*
*'It' was never 'me',*
*was it?*
*Wasn't it?*
*My index finger holds its aim*
*like a ready-cocked gun*
*in case my words*
*weren't wounding enough.*
*Then, my eyes lower.*
*In that same accusing hand*
*are three fingers pointing back at me.*
*'Who sinned, Lord?*
*This man or his parents?'*
*'All have sinned and fallen short.'*
*'All who call on the name of the Lord*
*will be saved.'*
*The truth silences me.*
*Then sets us both free.*

# 17
# WHEN WE FEEL POWERLESS

**Then Asa called to the Lord his God and said, 'Lord, there is no one like you to help the powerless against the mighty. Help us, Lord our God, for we rely on you, and in your name we have come against this vast army. Lord, you are our God; do not let mere mortals prevail against you.'**
2 CHRONICLES 14:11

A key way we can be aware of our weakness is when we are feeling powerless. Perhaps there's a sense of, 'I can't possibly do that!', or of feeling we have no voice. Maybe things are happening that we have no control over, and all we can do is stand and watch. How precious it is that God sees and knows and understands. He never overlooks us or disregards our value.

When Moses received the commission to lead the enslaved Israelites into freedom at the burning bush, he felt vastly underqualified for the task: 'But Moses said to God, "Who am I that I should go to Pharaoh and bring the Israelites out of Egypt?"' (Exodus 3:11). It's a classic case of 'imposter syndrome', fearing that our weakness and inability will be exposed and ridiculed. The ensuing conversation between Moses and God is one that many of us have mimicked ever since. God explaining and persuading; Moses (us) trying to wriggle off the hook, ultimately protesting, 'Please send someone else' (Exodus 4:13).

Avoidance doesn't have to be the answer, though. Sometimes our weakness is the very thing that gives God the opportunity to do something new in us. When I first began living on my own, I found that my mental preparation had only got me so far. The reality was rather different. How would I cope with no one to talk to, no one to help me? I was speaking my prayers out loud when I heard myself say this: 'Grow me, Lord!' It had never even been in my mind before, but it hit the spot. I was fearful, vulnerable, and feeling inadequate; but instead of saying, 'Get me out of here' (which is what I felt), I'd said, 'Grow me', and that's just what God did. For the record, it's what he did for Moses, too, without him asking! It's been one of my favourite prayers ever since.

God-given strength is always a positive thing, and it differs from any strength we might try to develop ourselves or that we see around us. God intends to equip us to thrive in life and do good, rather different from how people can use strength (or perceived strength) as a weapon against others. We all learn, instinctively from a young age, that there is a pecking order in society: some people will become bosses, while others will be the underdogs, with a complex hierarchy in between. People use their strength as a way of asserting superiority. I'm sure I'm not the only one who doesn't like being told what to do, as there's a subconscious drive in many of us to become the person on top, the one who does the telling. At its worst, we see some taking their power in dark directions, becoming bullies, abusers, and manipulators, while some of us unwittingly become their victims.

Is this what we aspire to when we seek to become stronger – to somehow be seen as better than everyone else?

Surely we have to say an emphatic 'No' to that.

What about those times we feel that things are getting out of our control or someone is making us do something against our will? When our opinion is disregarded or not even listened to? When what we want or need is dismissed as irrelevant and unimportant?

Perhaps your landlord has decided to sell the property you're renting. It's been the heart of your family's life, but now you have two months to find something else and get out.

Your company has just been taken over – first you have heard about it – and the new owners want a fresh start. After everything you have done for them, you are facing redundancy.

Your adult child announces they are taking a job in another part of the country (or even halfway across the world).

With only weeks to go, your fiancé(e) has had a change of heart and called off the wedding.

Someone has made a false allegation against you, and it's looking like it's going to end up in the hands of the police.

These are just a handful of real examples from people I know and, no doubt, we can think of other situations we and our loved ones have faced. In every one of them, there is a sense of injustice along with the powerlessness. It isn't right! Don't I have a say in the matter? What about me?! Is no one listening? But instead of jumping up and down, demanding our rights, again I'm going to gently suggest that there's another way.

Surrender.

Hear me carefully, though. I'm not meaning that we should 'cave in' or resign ourselves to 'never having what we want'. (This is especially important when the person we are dealing with is behaving with deliberate, harmful intent.) But it's definitely a case of laying down our own agenda and saying to God, 'Your will be done.'

It seems counterintuitive, but it's in those times of surrender that we can find a strength we never thought possible. The world's way would be to try to outsmart our opponent or deliver a killer comeback, but this is only playing into the whole power struggle we want to avoid. God, though, has a soft spot for the underdog, the persecuted, the disadvantaged. And he never asks us to do something that he didn't already model.

> **He withdrew about a stone's throw beyond them, knelt down and prayed, 'Father, if you are willing, take this cup from me; yet not my will, but yours be done.' An angel from heaven appeared to him and strengthened him. And being in anguish, he prayed more earnestly, and his sweat was like drops of blood falling to the ground.**
>
> LUKE 22:41–44

Submitting to the injustice of a rigged trial, the cruelty of torture, and the agony of the cross was not weakness. No human being – however powerful – had the right to kill the Son of God: 'No one takes [my life] from me, but I lay it down of my own accord' (John 10:18). Jesus faced all that on our behalf, because he knew his mission and was utterly secure in his Father's love.

Thank God we are not called to endure such terrors as those! But in the things we do suffer at the hands of other people, we can know that same security. In yielding to his Lordship, not only can we survive the suffering, but we can receive a peace, blessing, and strength within it all that turns the world's way on its head. Paul taught this same lesson to the Corinthian church. He wrote:

> **But God chose the foolish things of the world to shame the wise; God chose the weak things of the world to shame the strong.**
>
> 1 CORINTHIANS 1:27

He himself deliberately laid down his education and his speaking skills in order to become powerless, so that God's power would be demonstrated:

> **For I resolved to know nothing while I was with you except Jesus Christ and him crucified. I came to you in weakness with great fear and trembling.**
>
> 1 CORINTHIANS 2:2–3

What a challenge for us to consider!

## Response

Spend a few moments thinking of God's greatness and reminding yourself of his power. Express it in song if you like.

Lay before him the things you're facing that have rendered you powerless, then yield yourself to him afresh.

*Lord, without you I am nothing. I choose to surrender to you today, so that you become everything to me. Be my strength, my shield, my defender. Come through for me, God, and grow me in those areas I am weak. For your glory, Amen.*

For further reflection and worship, listen to 'I speak Jesus' by Charity Gayle.

## Evening reflection: Through a different lens

*God, I am not able*
*to stand unless you hold me,*
*to speak unless you give me voice.*
*I cannot think with clarity*
*nor demonstrate real wisdom*
*unless you first inspire.*
*This knowledge of my feebleness*
*comes with blessed relief:*
*without you I am nothing,*
*but since I am never without you,*
*I am never nothing.*
*Others may forget me,*
*disregard and sideline me;*
*events may overtake me,*
*threaten and engulf me.*
*But God…*
*Ever mindful of me,*
*watching over me,*
*safeguarding and protecting,*
*listening and cherishing.*
*In this,*
*in you, God,*
*I rest in peace.*

# 18

# LAMENT: GIVING LOSS A VOICE

**'How I long for the months gone by, for the days when God watched over me, when his lamp shone on my head and by his light I walked through darkness! Oh, for the days when I was in my prime, when God's intimate friendship blessed my house, when the Almighty was still with me and my children were around me, when my path was drenched with cream and the rock poured out for me streams of olive oil.'**

JOB 29:2–6

**Hear my prayer, Lord; let my cry for help come to you. Do not hide your face from me when I am in distress. Turn your ear to me; when I call, answer me quickly.**

PSALM 102:1–2

Today, we're turning to look at loss, whether caused through life's inevitabilities, our own carelessness, or by something or someone being stolen from us. Putting the pain of loss into words can be so hard, but expressing our grief helps ease our inner pain as we offer it all to God and seek his help in bringing us through.

I grew up in a home where you weren't supposed to make a fuss. If I cried when a toy got broken, the response would be either, 'What are you crying for, it's only a ________________?' or the charming, 'Stop crying or I'll give you something to cry about.' The baseline message was: it wasn't important. It didn't matter to my parents, so it shouldn't matter to me. As we have observed in chapter 5, it's a very small step – barely a twitch – from saying 'It doesn't matter' to 'You don't matter'.

Part of our response to loss, then, may lie in changing the narrative we have been living with. The new message, spoken gently with compassion and kindness, becomes: 'What I have lost matters. It really matters to me.' I don't mean to imply that we only need a psychological fix (what counsellors call 'reframing' or 'cognitive restructuring'), that to name our issue differently will sort everything out. We can call it whatever we like, and label it in any number of convincing ways, but the point is that what we really, really need is honesty.

And God really, really wants to hear it.

The loss we're struggling to process might be our health. Our body is letting us down. We can't do the things we used to do. Perhaps the GP is telling us, 'It's just your age,' but there's no 'just' about it. In fact, it doesn't feel just at all.

Perhaps it's the loss of a relationship, whether that's a marriage or a friendship or that sense that our grown-up children don't need us anymore. We are hardwired for connection, and when those connections become loose, when the two parts no longer fit together, we feel its loss at a cellular level. It's for a good reason we call it a broken heart. When the relationship has ended through bereavement, the loss is compounded. I needn't say more.

Maybe it's a job that's been lost, or an opportunity, or the sense of self-worth we used to get from what we did and who we were. It can feel like an axe has struck repeatedly, leaving us cut down, diminished, no longer fruitful.

I know that some people seem to be able to shrug off difficult circumstances, bouncing back so soon after being felled, but I have a theory about that. I think they are in denial. The Kübler-Ross model of the five stages of grief is a little outmoded now, but we can still recognise, I think, that our initial instinct is usually to deny either what has happened or the enormity of it. As an optimist, I can see how it has played out at various stages of my life. 'Oh, it's not so bad!' or 'Oh well, never mind! Could be worse!' might be appropriate if I've scorched the apple crumble, but it absolutely doesn't apply to any life circumstance that takes some processing. You see, if we only squash down how we are feeling, we miss all of that vital 'working through it' and – most dangerously of all – we avoid bringing God into it or bringing it to God. That strategy might spare us some pain in the short-term but will wreak havoc eventually. Thankfully, the Bible teaches us a better way, that of lament, which can be defined as 'expressing sorrow and grief over travesty, injustices, sicknesses, death, or other brokenness within a fallen world'.[5]

Let's walk through its steps together, just reading them through for now, then taking some practical steps at the end.

As we have said, the first thing is to acknowledge with honesty the loss we are lamenting. We are giving it a name, if it doesn't have one already, to reinforce the awful reality. We have not made it up. We are not making a 'fuss about nothing'. It does matter.

Secondly, we need to take time to sit with it, an essential part of learning to grieve. It is not enough to name it and rush on, without so much as a proper introduction. After my younger son left home, I spent some time just riffling my fingers through his vast Lego collection. As I went to get up, I sensed a voice saying, 'Will you not just sit with me?' Sometimes grief needs to be our companion.

The third step is to let the feelings come. *Let* them come. We may not have control over what happens to us, but we can always choose our responses (if not our reactions, which are more instinctive). If we usually repress our emotions to keep ourselves nicely in denial, it might take some time for them to bubble up. Whether that's sadness, anger, or whatever, they will find their way to the surface (and to the exit), so long as we don't get in their way.

The psalms are full of examples of the writer pouring out their pain and frustration in all its rawness, but it rarely stops there. The beautiful thing is that, when all that honesty and the accompanying emotions are expressed, there is suddenly room for God to step in. When the raging stops, the peace can start. When the tears are spent, hope rises up.

I urge you to try it.

Give voice to your loss through lament.

It will stop you being stuck.

It's the start of freedom and of strength.

## Response

At your own pace, begin to work through the steps we just read. Every tiny step will bring benefit, so don't worry if you can't do much at a time. It's a good idea to write your thoughts down, to encourage further processing.

Begin in the stillness, inviting God to come. Don't worry about not being able to find the right words, as God can hear our hearts. The Bible tells us that the Holy Spirit prays on our behalf, using 'groans that words cannot express' (Romans 8:26, GNB). You could also sing it. If it is helpful, use the following prayer to get started:

*God, it's hard to face up to loss when it feels I have lost so much. I've tried to cope, tried to pray – you know I have – but mostly I have only succeeded in burying it alive. Please send your Holy Spirit to be my counsellor and helper, so I can learn to do it your way. Guide me step by step so I can be healed and free. Amen.*

These verses may also prove helpful:

> **When life is heavy and hard to take, go off by yourself. Enter the silence. Bow in prayer. Don't ask questions: Wait for hope to appear. Don't run from trouble. Take it full-face. The 'worst' is never the worst.**
> LAMENTATIONS 3:28–30 (MSG)

> **You keep track of all my sorrows. You have collected all my tears in your bottle. You have recorded each one in your book. My enemies will retreat when I call to you for help. This I know: God is on my side!**
> PSALM 56:8–9 (NLT)

For further reflection and worship, listen to 'Broken vessels (Amazing grace)' by Hillsong Worship.

## Evening reflection: Only the best will do

*You say, O Lord, that*
*so precious are our tears to you,*
*that you store them in a bottle –*
*one of exquisite cut-glass*
*or finest crystal.*
*Only the best will do.*
*You stand – I imagine – with it outstretched, ready,*
*because you know how much of life makes us weep.*
*I see it as wide-rimmed*
*for when the drops cascade in free-flow*
*rather than merely drip,*
*and of infinite capacity,*
*more's the pity.*
*Yet there are many times,*
*too many to count,*
*when the tears will not come,*
*when it is safer, better, simpler all round*
*to deny them.*
*What if we start and then cannot stop,*
*a dam bursting in our fractured heart?*
*Could there possibly be a bottle big enough?*
*Then I remember – and therefore have hope –*
*that it is we who come with limits*
*and not you, O God.*
*There is a time to mourn*
*and an end to grief,*
*though it may be too far off yet to discern.*
*The night presses in, its darkness all around,*
*but joy comes in the morning*
*and to this, and to you, Lord,*
*we will cling.*

# 19

# REACHING THE TIPPING POINT

**'Go and look toward the sea,' he told his servant. And he went up and looked. 'There is nothing there,' he said. Seven times Elijah said, 'Go back.' The seventh time the servant reported, 'A cloud as small as a man's hand is rising from the sea.'**

1 KINGS 18:43–44

**Let perseverance finish its work so that you may be mature and complete, not lacking anything.**

JAMES 1:4

*'Tipping point, noun: the point at which the number of small changes over a period of time reaches a level where a further small change has a sudden and very great effect on a system.'*[6]

From all the stories I heard as a child in school assembly, one stands out in my memory. I don't even know if it is true, though Miss Clancy said it was. She described an iron girder, suspended by chains from a beam. Then she said that a cork attached to a string was rigged up somehow to be continually swung mechanically against the girder: donk… donk… donk… I don't remember how long she said it took, but eventually the tipping point was reached: the iron bar surrendered to the constant assault and began to swing.

Or imagine an old-fashioned set of scales and weights. If you put an eight-ounce weight on one pan, then pour sugar into the other one, when the pans are perfectly level you know that you have weighed out eight ounces of sugar. It's astonishing how just a few extra grains of sugar are enough to shift the balance beyond the 'tipping point' to move the pan in the other direction.

In a way, I needn't explain what we mean by the tipping point, since life teaches it almost daily. One minute we are just about coping with everything going on, then something happens: someone says something, or one of the children is sick, or we remember too late that we were supposed to be somewhere or do something, and suddenly everything caves in on us. We might call it 'the straw that breaks the camel's back': it doesn't matter how small it is, the point is it's *yet another thing*. And it's too much. Again.

So much of what we've been looking at so far, in terms of what weakens us and how hard life can be, is in this category. But the same principle of tiny things making a difference can apply in a positive direction. Can we, I wonder, begin to imagine a tipping point where weakness fades away and strength gains the upper hand?

Yet another image comes to mind: a playground see-saw. When two friends are of a similar size, it's an easy thing to get it going, but when a child is pitched against an adult, it's a very different story. The poor child is left suspended in mid-air, feet dangling, while the adult takes up permanent residence at ground level. Is this how we see the battle between weakness and strength? An uneven match? A foregone conclusion?

In starting to turn our thoughts towards change and improvement, several questions might arise. What would that change feel like? How would my life look in this new season? Perhaps chief of all, though, is: how will it happen? Will God answer our 'Give me strength!' prayer with a once-and-for-all decisive intervention; in other words, a miracle? He can, and does sometimes, for sure. But reading many stories in the Bible and the testimonies of believers through the ages, we have to conclude that God tends to lead us by a more circuitous route.

Before going further, let's be clear (again!) that we are still not venturing into 'self-help' territory. The whole point of this book is to lead us to

God, who is the source of our strength. As we have already said – and knew anyway – if we could change our lives and get ourselves sorted, we would have done it long before now. However, that said, reaching the tipping point will require step-by-step action. Thankfully, we don't even have to do that in our own strength, either.

Let's turn to the Bible, starting with that detail from the story of Elijah, quoted above. The drought came upon the nation of Israel suddenly, when God spoke through the prophet. Although it would have taken some time for the water-courses to dry up, the rain stopped coming as soon as that word was delivered. For a drought to end, you need rain again, and for that you need cloud. When Elijah told his servant to look out to sea, he didn't say what he was looking for. Each time he gave his blank report he was urged to go again. He must have wondered what he was missing. Finally, with perhaps a shrug and a rolling of his eyes, he went for a seventh time and saw what Elijah knew in his spirit was coming: a tiny cloud rising from the horizon.

Do you sense the power of hope in that appearance?

The consequences of drought of any kind – when something is lacking in our lives day after day – are enormous. We are thirsty. We are fruitless. We are exhausted from the slog. And perhaps we are wearied from praying so often for something to change. That cloud 'as small as a man's hand' signalled the start of the tipping point. Oh, I grant you, it didn't look like it but it was enough for Elijah to get moving, quickly, before the rain stopped him. That cloud spread across the skies, ever-darkening with its threat of downpour, until the heavens opened. Let us never despise the day of small beginnings (Zechariah 4:10). Change has to start somewhere.

Another example is the story of Naaman the Syrian (found in 2 Kings 5). He was miraculously healed of leprosy after (eventually) obeying Elisha's instruction to bathe in the river Jordan seven times, but not before complaining about the method.

> **Naaman went away angry and said, 'I thought that he would surely come out to me and stand and call on the name of the Lord his God, wave his hand over the spot and cure me of my leprosy.'**
> 2 KINGS 5:11

He thought, as we do ourselves, that an instant miracle would be so much easier. He must have struggled to understand how 'washing' in a dirty river could possibly achieve anything – and the first few times, that's exactly what resulted. But he 'went again'. He dipped himself under for a seventh time, and then the miracle happened.

Why does God lead us like this? I don't have all the answers, but I know he loves to invite us into partnership with him. What would our faith be like – and, indeed, our relationship with him – if all we had to do was metaphorically press a button for God to act in just the way we needed him to? And as for why we have to wait (and wait, and wait) sometimes, again there are no easy answers. But when we get to the tipping point, to the moment when something shifts and change happens, the wait is worth it. As the verse above says: 'Let perseverance finish its work so that you may be mature and complete, not lacking anything' (James 1:4).

If you're desperate for something to change, do not lose heart.

Go again!

You might be nearer to the tipping point than you realise.

Change is possible.

And it's coming.

## Response

Spend some time in prayer, perhaps writing down your thoughts and reflections as you do.

If you can, draw a picture of some old-fashioned scales. What is on each pan? What do you think needs to happen for the balance to tip in your circumstances?

Is there something specific you need to pray for?

Does a verse or a promise come to mind?

Commit all these things to God, in Jesus' name.

For further reflection and worship, listen to 'God, turn it around' by Jon Reddick.

## Evening reflection: Not my way, but yours

*Would I bathe in a muddy river*
*if my God gave the word?*
*Would I endure any hardship*
*if he urged that I should?*
*Could he not simply utter*
*and a miracle be born?*
*Do I have to go on fighting*
*when I'm already battle-worn?*

*The path of least resistance*
*is the one I'd always choose,*
*where my ankles would never turn*
*and my way I'd never lose.*
*I'd leave my pain behind me*
*as I strode my way ahead;*
*hoping, though still doubting,*
*that the past was good as dead.*

*But life has often shown me*
*this is not the Saviour's way.*
*His lessons don't come easy*
*and demand that we must pray,*
*not for simple and quick fixes*
*that will patch our wounded soul*
*but for total restoration,*
*a life made fully whole.*

# SECTION II

# Finding strength in God

# 20

# GOD: A FORTRESS TO PROTECT THE WEAK

**God is our refuge and strength, an ever-present help in trouble.**
PSALM 46:1

**My God is my rock, in whom I take refuge, my shield and the horn of my salvation. He is my stronghold, my refuge and my saviour – from violent people you save me.**
2 SAMUEL 22:3

**The name of the Lord is a fortified tower; the righteous run to it and are safe.**
PROVERBS 18:10

**How priceless is your unfailing love, O God! People take refuge in the shadow of your wings.**
PSALM 36:7

I have a clear memory from when I was about six, when one Saturday afternoon there was a thunderstorm. I wasn't particularly bothered by it, because I'd heard someone in the playground say it meant that God was just 'rearranging the furniture', but the house was in a gloom as deep as nightfall. As I went into one of the unoccupied downstairs rooms to fetch something, I reached up for the light switch at just the moment the next flash of lightning came. The room lit up before I had activated the switch, and this display of what felt like black magic absolutely terrified me. I ran into the sitting room and landed on my mum's lap, aware of her flinging her knitting to one side so I didn't impale myself in the process. I couldn't answer her repeated, 'What's the matter? What's happened?' All I could do was sob and cling on to her until I felt better.

Today we are going to look at one of the key biblical descriptions of God's strength: that he is our refuge, our shelter, the one we instinctively run to when we are in trouble. And I say 'instinctively' because even those who claim to profess no faith, or who refuse to acknowledge God's existence at all, can find themselves praying when crisis hits. We may not understand what we are doing sometimes, but we find ourselves running to him just the same.

It's always important to root our thinking in what the Bible actually says, rather than letting our experiences dictate what we believe. Put it this way, we have already highlighted again and again how our opinions about our weakness can be skewed, so it's altogether possible that our perspective on God's strength might be a bit off, too. The verses quoted above are just a small selection of what the Bible offers us, but they are a great starting point, so that we can learn to recognise God's strength when we see it.

It's no surprise that the word 'run' appears in the list. Seeking out refuge implies we are in trouble, so I don't imagine we would be casually sauntering towards it. If we are out when the storm clouds gather, and we spot something – anything – in the distance that might serve as a shelter, we make a dash for it, hopefully before we get drenched. Or if someone is chasing us, we would be running as fast as we can, hoping to either outrun our pursuer or to duck unnoticed into a crevice that will hide us. Note that whatever scenario we're imagining, we run with hope. Fear might be driving us from behind, but hope encourages us forward.

Let's explore first of all the image of God as a strong tower. I wonder how we picture it in our minds? Is it distant? On a hill some way off? Do we imagine it as being fortified and guarded, or is it abandoned? Thankfully, the Bible offers nothing at all negative in this description. This strong tower is God himself. We are not seeking shelter and refuge in 'it' but in 'him'. In fact, the Proverbs verse above says 'the name of the Lord is a fortified tower', and I take that to mean that even calling out 'Jesus! Help me!' is enough to bring us into a place of safety. This is of great comfort when we feel too tired to run, too exhausted to make the effort.

The name of Jesus is always sufficient.

God is always enough.

Note, too, that the refuge-that-is-God is grounded on rock. When everything seems shaken around us, when we feel our legs wobble and our feet start to slip, he is the rock underneath us that holds us steady. If we feel like we are about to go under, with wave upon wave of difficulty breaking over our head, our feet can find a solid ledge to keep us from drowning. The rock is our sure foundation and the fortress is our solid protection all around us. We are shielded on all sides by impenetrable rock.

It's a great image, but as we all know from our own times of crisis and trouble, it's not just security we need, but comfort. Happily, the Bible portrays God's shelter in wonderfully warm ways, too. When my friend had to leave her home to escape domestic violence, she arrived at the doors of the women's refuge with nothing but her children and two supermarket bags' worth of possessions. This was no rock tower, just an ordinary semi-detached house in a suburban street, but inside she felt safer than she had in years. On the wall was a painting, done by one of the volunteers, of a hen with its chicks held close to her under her wings. My friend would grip one of the crocheted cushions to her stomach, staring at this picture, as she began her journey towards the God who had rescued her.

Finding refuge in 'the shadow of God's wings' is like being hugged within a mother's embrace. In fact, the Hebrew phrase 'El Shaddai', often used of God in the Old Testament, usually translated 'God Almighty' or 'God, all-sufficient', has its roots in the word 'shad' meaning 'breast', conveying a side of God that is both comforting and nurturing.

There is a softness in the description of 'the shadow of God's wings', an invitation to draw close to the one who never lets us go. It's a picture of compassion and love expressed with tenderness. The fortress may be strong and safe, but it's impersonal and has hard edges. The shadow of God's wings, though, offers every bit the same level of protection for us, his little ones who are vulnerable and hurting, and we are close enough to feel his warmth and hear his heartbeat.

I remember seeing on the news that after a forest fire had finally burned itself out, a bird was found with its wings stretched over her chicks. They had survived because of her willing sacrifice. There had been no way that she was going to put her little ones in danger. Likewise, with outstretched arms on a cross, our Saviour gave up his life also, for our sake. This is protection that we can depend on.

To sum up, God stands as this strong tower, this solid place of refuge, but it's not a forbidding, 'keep away' image. There's no sense that its doors are locked from the inside, that the safety is not available to us. It's not like a castle that demands a huge entrance fee. There's a sign on the wall that reads:

> **'Come to me, all you who are weary and burdened, and I will give you rest. Take my yoke upon you and learn from me, for I am gentle and humble in heart, and you will find rest for your souls. For my yoke is easy and my burden is light.'**
> MATTHEW 11:28–30

When we look up, we see him standing with arms ready to draw us into embrace, and saying, 'I've been waiting for you to come.'

## Response

Read through Psalm 91, which is full of descriptions of God's protection of us.

Write down the ones which speak to you the most, drawing a picture if you find that helpful.

Then spend a few moments in quietness, accepting God's invitation for you to nestle under his wing. Receive his strength as an infusion, and enjoy new depths of peace and contentment.

For further reflection and worship, listen to 'God is for us' by CityAlight.

## Evening reflection: Our constant refuge

*When is it time to run for cover,*
*to seek the comfort of shelter?*
*When the heavens have broken open*
*to deliver their deluge*
*in one, overwhelming strike?*
*Or when the storm is yet circling,*
*a black-clouded beast on the prowl?*
*Is it better to anticipate –*
*to break rank from those*
*who say, 'It's nothing' –*
*and hide at the merest hint*
*of trouble in the skies?*
*Which choice would be the braver –*
*or the bolder –*
*the foolish –*
*or the wise?*
*Surely wisest still is to have no need of running*
*for we have stayed ever close to the Master's side.*
*His protecting arms are shield enough*
*for any threat of harm.*
*He is our refuge,*
*he is our strength,*
*in each and every season.*
*Why wait for storms at all,*
*when his refuge can be our home?*

# 21

# GOD IS STRONG, THROUGH AND THROUGH

> **Know therefore that the Lord your God is God; he is the faithful God, keeping his covenant of love to a thousand generations of those who love him and keep his commandments.**
> DEUTERONOMY 7:9

> **'Be strong and courageous. Do not be afraid or terrified because of them, for the Lord your God goes with you; he will never leave you nor forsake you.'**
> DEUTERONOMY 31:6

Yesterday, we looked at God's strength being represented as a tower, a safe refuge that is rock-solid, ever-present, and offering comfort to the weak. Today, we'll be going a little further, exploring what it is about God's characteristics – who he is through and through – that make him a source of strength for us. Just like a stick of rock, if we were to cut God in half, all his excellent qualities would run right through it.

In our own lives, I hope we can all recall people who have felt safe and strong for us. Our parents should have been our earliest expression of safety, providing for our every need and reassuring our tender, vulnerable lives simply through their presence. If we have gone on to have close friends, they have offered the added value of choosing us and accepting us for who we are. That firm foundation then gives us courage to confide in them our deepest thoughts and feelings. Other relationships offer security in other ways: our boss, validating our skills and rewarding our efforts; our medical teams; even our hairdresser, when you come to think about it. In short, these are people we can trust and dare to be vulnerable with.

It's often the case, as ever, that we have to learn tough lessons the hard way. When we're mistreated by those who should have cared for us; when we're betrayed by a friend or, worse still, a spouse; when we're passed over for promotion or made redundant with no warning; when our symptoms are dismissed. All these, and the many more examples we could mention, go to serve how fragile the apparent stability they offered really is, and how disappointingly weak was the strength we thought we were relying on.

Before going further, let's indulge in a moment of 'What if?' Consider for a moment if God were a politician or leader of a nation. He would likely then do as they all seem to: issue his manifesto and present it so winningly that we are all persuaded to vote him into office, only for him to immediately renege on his promise, backtrack, and explain how things 'really were'. Instead of offering strength and stability, and encouraging trust, this produces the very opposite. Not only has that version of God let us down, but we also become cynical, knowing we could never trust him for anything else ever again.

Thank God he is not like that!

My image of a strong person is one who can physically carry me when I'm unable to take another step; who can support me emotionally, coping with my outbursts, my anger, my fears, my tears and tantrums, and my complaining; who can listen to my stories over and over and not reject me for it; who can love me despite my giving them every reason not to. It sounds a tall order, but this is where God really stands out from the crowd.

If this were some sort of dating site, and the list of essentials for our 'ideal match' went along the lines of the above, we would be dismissed as delusional. But God really is that perfect and we can trust the Bible's description of God and his character. God doesn't age, doesn't wear out, doesn't change, and never fails – the list goes on. At any point in our lives, we can lean our full weight on him and he will not drop us.

If we are to understand anything today – really take it deeply into our hearts and minds – it's that God is not like anyone else. As we go through some of the ways now that he presents his strength to us through his character, we may find memories coming up of people who have not treated us so well. If that's the case, feel free to pause often, bringing each stab of pain to him.

> **Before the mountains were born or you brought forth the whole world, from everlasting to everlasting you are God.**
> PSALM 90:2

In a world where nothing lasts, this is a truth we need to drink deeply from. The concept of eternity is almost impossible for our finite minds to get round, but we live in the benefit of it every day. While friends and family come and go, through changing circumstances or because of bereavement, and destabilising us in the meantime, God will absolutely be around forever and ever. If we've ever received a card or letter signed off with 'Forever yours', only to then later lose that person, we must take heart that when God says that, he means it.

> **'Be strong and courageous. Do not be afraid or terrified because of them, for the Lord your God goes with you; he will never leave you nor forsake you.'**
> DEUTERONOMY 31:6

This is a one-step-further benefit of his eternal existence: he is always present with us. We need never feel alone for a single moment. In our frailty, we can believe we are on our own, but this promise is one we can lean on.

> **Know therefore that the Lord your God is God; he is the faithful God, keeping his covenant of love to a thousand generations of those who love him and keep his commandments.**
> DEUTERONOMY 7:9

If we've ever known the horror of having a confidence broken – and, sadly, I can't imagine a person who hasn't – then this promise comes as great reassurance. Has a friend ever let us down? God never will. He is faithful. This is part of his very essence.

> **'I the Lord do not change. So you, the descendants of Jacob, are not destroyed.'**
> MALACHI 3:6

> **Jesus Christ is the same yesterday and today and forever.**
> HEBREWS 13:8

This one was worth saying twice! We don't need to check whether God is in a good mood today. He is stable in every aspect of who he is and what he does. We can depend on him loving us today, tomorrow, and all the days ahead.

> **Good and upright is the Lord; therefore he instructs sinners in his ways.**
> PSALM 25:8

This is no act, no 'being on his best behaviour to win you over'. God is good and he behaves perfectly well, all the time.

There are so many verses we could pull up to find more examples of God's wonderful perfection, but hopefully this has gone some way in getting the message across.

He is strong for us because he doesn't come and go, blow hot and cold, say one thing and mean another, throw our words back in our faces, let us down, fail to turn up, or prove to be a phoney.

God is the real deal. We can lean our whole weight on him. He is strength personified.

## Response

Which aspects of God's character mean the most to you at the moment?

Thank him for being that way for you, perhaps turning some of your thoughts into a song.

*God almighty, eternal, ever-present, and ever-loving, we turn to you in our weakness, sin, and self-sufficiency and pray that you infuse us with your attributes. We want to be more like you, in order to live well, demonstrate your goodness to those around us, and give glory to you. Amen.*

For further reflection and worship, listen to 'Goodness of God' by Bethel Music.

## Evening reflection: More than the sum of its letters

*Omnipresent,*
*omniscient,*
*omnipotent;*
*words I learned a lifetime ago,*
*to spell,*
*or to unpick from Latin.*
*But God is not a matter of mere words,*
*however fancy*
*or incomprehensible.*
*Or if he is,*
*then they are simple ones*
*and backed up by everything he does:*
*he is good,*
*love,*
*here,*
*always,*
*faithful,*
*true,*
*mine.*
*These are not labels*
*that fade in the wash*
*or lose their adhesion.*
*These are the truths about God*
*that I stake my life upon,*
*lean my full weight against,*
*trade for life's sorrows,*
*any day,*
*forever and always.*

# 22

# HOW DO WE STRENGTHEN OURSELVES IN THE LORD?

**When David and his men reached Ziklag, they found it destroyed by fire and their wives and sons and daughters taken captive. So David and his men wept aloud until they had no strength left to weep. David's two wives had been captured – Ahinoam of Jezreel and Abigail, the widow of Nabal of Carmel. David was greatly distressed because the men were talking of stoning him; each one was bitter in spirit because of his sons and daughters. But David found strength in the Lord his God.**

1 SAMUEL 30:3–6

**'But when you pray, go into your room, close the door and pray to your Father, who is unseen. Then your Father, who sees what is done in secret, will reward you.'**

MATTHEW 6:6

Some years ago, I was on the last day of Wainwright's coast-to-coast walk, not too far from the final destination of Robin Hood's Bay. Despite my tiredness, there was a spring in my step, until I soon encountered a problem: a vast area of brackish bog between me and where I needed to go. My friends had pressed on ahead of me, as usual, and were waiting at a stile in the distance. Whichever way I looked, there was no obvious (dry or easy) place to tread on. The tufts of cotton-grass proved little help. I was stuck this side of it, and sure didn't want to get stuck *inside* of it! I called across to my friends: 'How did you get over there?'

It's the key question we need to start asking today. So far, we've considered a lot of 'whats' and a few 'whys'. I hope our reflections have gained us some insight and that perhaps we can spot signs of God starting to minister into our situations. We know the areas we are weak in, and we believe that God is supremely strong, but how do we bridge the gap – this no-clear-path-for-our-feet – between us and this strength that we desperately need? When the Bible says, 'David found strength in the Lord his God', what does it mean?

My friends didn't answer me that day. Perhaps they didn't hear me, for they kept chatting to themselves while they waited for me to catch up. I had to work it out myself. And this is how I'm going to tackle this and the remaining chapters. You won't find any glib answers, nor clichés for that matter. I can't even claim that the way I have learned to cross over into strength is the best way. We are all individuals, uniquely created, and there is never a one-size-fits-all answer. (Just a brief peek at the gospel narratives reveals how Jesus healed one person this way, another person another way. He still does that today.) All I am going to do is share how I did it and hope that God will show each one of us how and where to place our feet, too.

The verse from Matthew highlights the most important thing I learned to do when I needed strength: retreat to find privacy and be alone. Yes, I mean I took myself away from the people and situations I needed escape from. But it wasn't solitude I craved so much as the presence of the only one who understood: Jesus.

I was usually close to tears, my mind raging with all the things I needed to express but dared not voice.[7] I would drop to my knees, often with my forehead against the carpet, and cry: silent, throat-aching, mouth-wide-open screams. These were times of desperation, expressed to Jesus multiple times a week, like a child bursting in from a tough day at school and blurting it all out.

Most of my friends had no idea what agonies I was routinely dealing with, but I wouldn't have turned to them anyway. God was the only one who could give me what I needed. You see, I'm not describing 'getting it out of our system', though that has its benefits. Nor is it about getting some sympathy and comfort, which is lovely, too. It's about giving it to God, knowing – trusting, believing, hoping – that he can do something to make it better.

And he always did.

There were times like this when God spoke to me, as close to audibly as I could imagine. Once, something on the telly had been triggering, and I became upset. The person I was with chose that moment to make an insensitive comment, whereupon I left the room. As I walked upstairs, I asked God, 'Did you hear all that? [I knew that he had.] What would you have said?' In an instant I heard his reply: 'Come here, my darling.'

This, *this*, is finding strength.

Within other times of crisis, I have noticed what you may have spotted there or experienced yourself: God is incredibly kind. During the break-up of my marriage, for example, I didn't know that my husband was having an affair, but only knew that I found incredibly difficult the evenings he and my sons were down at the youth club (which 'she' ran), and I would turn to the Bible and pray. One particular night, I was reading Psalm 46 in *The Message*: 'God is a safe place to hide, ready to help when we need him. We stand fearless at the cliff-edge of doom, courageous in seastorm and earthquake' (vv. 1–3). I remember crying out: 'God, I'm *not* fearless at the cliff-edge. I'm terrified! I'm not courageous at all!' And before the words were barely out of my mouth, I sensed his words in almost audible reply: 'Then come close to me until you feel braver.'

Honestly, this reply shocked me. I thought God would tell me off, along the lines of Jesus criticising his disciples' lack of faith (Matthew 8:26). I didn't expect such kindness, such gentleness. It prepared the way for God offering deep, deep comfort when the adultery was eventually exposed and my marriage ended.

Back to my on-the-carpet times with God, and I had confidence that he cared very much for me. When I cried out for rescue, I never sensed his rebuke. When I would flip open the pages of my Bible, asking, 'When are you going to do something, Lord?', he was gracious enough to always give me a verse that held out hope. Rescue would come, I learned to know it; I just had to keep hunkering into him until it did.

Interacting with God in these 'getting alone with him' times has no formula. God has a wonderful way of speaking our language, using phrases or illustrations he knows we will understand. I suspect, though we can't be certain, that David 'found strength in the Lord' by singing a psalm or bringing to mind times when God had helped him previously. He might have spoken out loud God's attributes and urged his soul to take courage. Chief of all – and so utterly crucial – I don't doubt he would have spent time away from everyone else, simply being in God's presence.

There is a way across the bog.

We might get very wet feet – as I actually did that day – and it might be hard and messy, but there is a way.

## Response

Schedule some time to meet with God on your own. Block it out in your diary if you need to; make plans to leave the house, if it's the only way of guaranteeing peace and quiet.

Don't be anxious that God won't show up or that he'll be silent.

It's more likely the case that he's already there, waiting for you to come.

Let it all out.

No need to be polite.

Feel for his hand in the darkness of your agonies and don't let go.

And don't be in a hurry to move on.

He has all the time in the world.

For further reflection and worship, listen to 'Strength will rise (Everlasting God)' by Chris Tomlin.

## Evening reflection: In David's echo

*I'm no David on a hillside*
*playing his harp as he kept vigil*
*over the flock in his care.*
*But, like him, I cast my eyes heavenward,*
*resolutely,*
*frequently,*
*away from life's troubles.*
*I echo the shepherd boy's cry,*
*'My heart says of you,*
*"Seek his face!"'**
*Yes, Lord, your face do I seek,*
*through tough hours of the day*
*and long watches of the night.*
*Only in your temple –*
*in whatever guise it appears –*
*can I find the peace,*
*the strength,*
*the rest*
*I crave.*
*And surely David's boast is mine, too,*
*that the goodness and mercy of God*
*shall follow me all the days –*
*and nights –*
*of my life*
*and I will dwell in the house of the Lord,*
*in his calming presence,*
*not only now and the day ahead*
*but forever.*

*Psalm 27:8

# 23
# FINDING STRENGTH THROUGH CONNECTION

> **'Remain in me, as I also remain in you. No branch can bear fruit by itself; it must remain in the vine. Neither can you bear fruit unless you remain in me.'**
> JOHN 15:4

> **'I am the vine; you are the branches. Whoever abides in me and I in him, he it is that bears much fruit, for apart from me you can do nothing.'**
> JOHN 15:5 (ESV)

We looked in chapter 14 at loneliness and isolation and how living under those conditions affects us. Now, as our thoughts turn increasingly to not just seeking but finding and keeping strength in God, it will be helpful to look at what the Bible has to say about connection.

At a leaders' prayer meeting, one of our youth workers was about to bring some teaching on this topic. She arrived with a stem from her vine, cut minutes before she left home, and laid it in the middle of the floor. We did our usual sharing, praying, and worshipping, then she led us through her prepared content. It was only an hour or so after the branch had been cut that I reached down to pick it up for her. I struggled to take in what it had become. In such a short space of time it was limp, hanging from my fingers like no more than a piece of rope, its leaves buckling in on themselves.

Sometimes we have to see something with our own eyes before we can properly take it in.

How many times have we heard or read the words of Jesus quoted above, describing himself as the vine and us as the branches? And how often has our response been on the dismissive side: agreeing with its sentiments, for sure, but quickly moving on?

Now I have seen that healthy vine branch rendered useless and pathetic so soon after being severed from its parent, I can never again read these words so flippantly. I had always interpreted them in terms of fruitfulness, of productivity, but actually it is more basic than that: a branch needs connection just to exist at all.

I'd like to think that in a previous generation, perhaps only 50 or so years ago, we wouldn't have needed the same kind of lesson. Families lived just doors from each other, able to follow that ancient hypothesis, 'It takes a village to raise a child'. People stayed in jobs for life, forming enduring friendships alongside the stability of a secure income. If you wanted a chat with someone, you popped round to their house, losing track of the hours as you shared together. I find myself wistful over that kind of easy connectiveness, comparing it with the impersonality of emails and texts, and the fact that, without even thinking it's odd, I have to arrange an audio or video call with a friend in advance.

But we don't need to restate the problems. We know only too well that the vast majority of us are living our lives in our own bubbles, but how do we break free of this individualism? How do we relearn what our forebears used to know? How can we reconnect with biblical truth in this area, and indeed, with God himself – in order that we can thrive within that connection?

Terry Waite was a special envoy to the Archbishop of Canterbury when in 1987, on a mission to Lebanon, he was captured by Hezbollah (the Lebanese Shia Islamist political party and paramilitary group) and imprisoned for 1,763 days, almost five years. For almost the whole of that time, he was held in solitary confinement, chained to a wall for all but ten minutes of each day. That he survived at all is remarkable, given how physically ill he became at times; but the greater marvel is how he didn't go completely mad from having no one to talk to and nothing to distract him.

He has given many interviews since his release and written books on his experience, in which he reveals some of the things that helped him cope. Chief of all, and no surprise, is that he drew on his Christian faith and his belief that God was with him. He had no physical Bible to read, but treasured its truths in his heart and mind. Interestingly, he describes turning to formal prayers from well-learned liturgy rather than falling back on extempore praying:

> I felt in my psychological condition at the time, any prayers would be, 'Oh God, get me out of here!' But I don't believe God put me in there. So I fell back on the language of the prayer book. Most mornings, I saved a little bread and water in my beaker and I said to myself the communion service. 'We do not presume...' and so on was all there, and I could say it. In my imagination I was taking part in this act with congregations across the world, in parts of England or America. I joined with them, using my imagination.[8]

Does it seem less faith-filled to use our imagination? Doesn't it reduce it to just 'making it up'? On the contrary, I think it takes extraordinary faith to be able to somehow look up and beyond the terrible circumstances we are in, to inwardly connect with a worldwide family of believers who, we believe by faith, are very much alive and well and, who knows, even praying for us. If we look to Terry Waite as an illustration, it's most certainly of the 'Now faith is confidence in what we hope for and assurance about what we do not see' (Hebrews 11:1) variety.

The chains that kept Terry fixed to the wall were visible signs of connection to his captors, but his constant prayers were what connected him to God, his source of strength.

What are we using to connect ourselves to God?

I could go off at a tangent here and start talking about an electrical plug and socket. It's not a bad analogy, given that we know how useless any kind of appliance is unless it's actually plugged in and switched on. But it differs in one significant detail from Jesus' description of the vine. Electrical goods are designed to be plugged in and unplugged. In fact, certain appliances – transformers and chargers, for example – need to be disconnected to avoid risk of fire. The branches of the vine, however, are intrinsically connected to the plant. They develop as a natural process of the plant's maturation: they are designed to be there. Each branch is entirely dependent upon the parent plant for its nutrition. The idea of disconnecting and reconnecting branches at will is a complete nonsense. (When Jesus does go on to talk about cutting branches out, it's in the context of pruning for the sake of greater fruitfulness.)

So, where does this leave us, in our journey towards finding strength in God?

A key take-away is that there is no room for striving here. The description of the vine is an organic one: we don't have to try to be a branch or strain in any way to somehow reach and grab hold of the vine.

Jesus is the vine.

We are the branches.

We are already in the deepest connection possible.

We are already privileged to draw all we need for life from Jesus.

So, let's abide in him – 'reside, dwell, continue, persist, remain steadfast' (OED)[9] – and let him do in and for us what he intended: that we thrive and be fruitful, drawing on his strength as naturally as breathing.

## Response

As you ponder these thoughts, doodle some drawings of a stem and branch with leaves, letting God speak to you through it.

Our prayer at one time might have been, 'Lord Jesus, come and live in my heart.'

How do you respond to God flipping that around and asking you to abide in him?

For further reflection and worship, listen to 'Draw me close' by Michael W. Smith.

## Evening reflection: True connection

*I thought it depended on me –*
*holding your hand tight,*
*locking your truths in my heart.*
*I saw connection, if I'm honest,*
*as a fragile thing,*
*my puny efforts no match*
*for storm or gusty wind.*
*I thought all of it depended on me –*
*my behaviour,*
*my attitudes,*
*my actions,*
*all betraying how closely – or not –*
*I followed you.*
*But my ears are open to the truth,*
*my eyes observant:*
*you are the Vine,*
*we all are the branches.*
*I am not the fragile leaf*
*about to be swept away,*
*crushed underfoot.*
*I am held*
*not by effort nor by striving,*
*but choosing to remain*
*where you have established me.*
*You are holding me:*
*you, the instigator and sustainer;*
*me, the one who rests and remains.*

# 24
# FINDING STRENGTH THROUGH HOLDING ON

**'I am coming soon. Hold on to what you have...'**
REVELATION 3:11

Over the next two days we're going to be looking at another aspect of connection: the idea of holding. Today, we'll consider who and what we should hold on to.

'Hold on...'

It usually means little more than 'wait a minute'; but how about this scenario? We've fallen into fast-moving water when we hear the yell, 'Hold on to this!' as someone throws us a lifebelt. We would surely grab that thing and hold on as if our life depended on it. Which, of course, it literally does.

In the autumn of 2005, I travelled to the south of England for a healing retreat. I was in a pretty bad way, mentally, and this was a last-ditch attempt at getting better. On one of the evenings, the team were sharing words of knowledge for the attendees. When it came to my turn, they pictured a deep pit – it didn't need describing, I'd been living in it for a while – and then a ladder being lowered into it. In my exhaustion and hopelessness, it felt like the last straw: now I was expected to climb my way out of the mess I was in. When I shared this reaction with my helper the next morning, she was shocked. 'But, Jane, don't you see? Jesus was coming down the ladder to lift you out!' Ah...

I wonder if you had a similar reaction when I said we were going to talk about holding on. Perhaps you have been holding out for prayers to be answered or holding on to a bad relationship in case the miracle does happen after all. We can all fill in our own gaps here. Some of us have been holding on for so long that our fingers are metaphorically cramped shut; we lost the feeling in them longer ago than we can remember. Perhaps you were hoping instead for a message of 'how to let go'? Well, that's not a bad first step to consider.

'Let go and let God' was a popular phrase on cards and posters back in the day. It's one thing to look at it sentimentally, though, and quite another to actually do it. Yet this is what we're talking about here: letting go of the things we've been holding on to – all of that 'in our own strength' stuff – and choosing to hold on to what is better; what can actually help.

> **'You have let go of the commands of God and are holding on to human traditions.'**
> MARK 7:8

Jesus is talking to the Pharisees here, when they had challenged the behaviour of his disciples in regard to ceremonial washing. Can we apply it to ourselves, I wonder? In our attempts to keep life and limb together, are we trusting in things of the self-help variety, instead of what God says? Are we so focused on reading the latest theory or science or running after the newest gadget, that we haven't actually read the Bible in ages? It's shocking how we find ourselves sliding into these things, not helped by the amount of 'click-bait' constantly being thrown at us.

So, these are some of the dangers and principles, but let's now look at what the Bible tells us we should hold on to (as if it were a life-belt – which it is).

> **Then you will shine among them like stars in the sky as you hold firmly to the word of life.**
> PHILIPPIANS 2:15–16

Our Bibles are as essential to life as food and drink. In fact, as Jesus demonstrated in his wilderness testing, God's word is more sustaining than physical nourishment. And it is not only for our benefit: the witness shines powerfully to those around us. As an example of that, when my husband left the family, my 16-year-old son told me that watching me turn to the word and seeing how it helped me cope had a profound effect on him. Let's not leave our Bibles to gather dust while we mindlessly scroll next to it on our devices.

> **Hold on to instruction, do not let it go; guard it well, for it is your life.**
> PROVERBS 4:13

> **So then, brothers and sisters, stand firm and hold fast to the teachings we passed on to you, whether by word of mouth or by letter.**
> 2 THESSALONIANS 2:15

> **Holding on to faith and a good conscience, which some have rejected and so have suffered shipwreck with regard to the faith.**
> 1 TIMOTHY 1:19

Whether we've been Christians a short time or long, and regardless of how diligently or sporadically we've had a daily quiet time, we should be familiar with at least the basic teachings of our faith. The simplicity of the gospel message alone can be enough: that without Christ we are in a mess, dead in our sins, and have no hope; while accepting his sacrifice on the cross grants forgiveness of all our sin and gives us countless blessing in this life and the whole of eternity. Cling to this truth while blessings seem invisible; hold on tight even though you think you've blown it; stand on the promises when life makes you wobble. Don't listen to any enemy taunts that so much as hint that you should be feeling guilty for what God has already dealt with.

> **Hold on to what is good.**
> 1 THESSALONIANS 5:21

This verse appears in the context of testing prophecies, but it's a great catch-all. If we've been holding on to some rubbish lately, it is a relief to put all that stinky stuff down and hold on to the good. I heard some teaching on Psalm 23 once, focusing on verse 2: 'He makes me lie down in green pastures.' The speaker said: 'Even if your green pasture looks like a mud swamp with one clump of grass in it, here is where you can rest.' So, if the good we're holding on to seems insubstantial, it's still worth it. Believe that there's more to come – not because it makes a good soundbite, but because God is that good.

Of course, holding on can also mean 'sticking it out', persevering, keeping on keeping on, as Paul highlights:

> **We also glory in our sufferings, because we know that suffering produces perseverance; perseverance, character; and character, hope.**
> ROMANS 5:3–4

Honestly, I always want to skip all of that and get straight to the character and hope part, but as we've seen already in chapter 19, that isn't how it works. We have to trust not just the process, but the God behind the process. If there was a better way of achieving our reward, he would show us one. All I know is that I have ended up grateful for every horrible situation I have been through, and I don't say that lightly.

> **Not that I have already obtained all this, or have already arrived at my goal, but I press on to take hold of that for which Christ Jesus took hold of me.**
> PHILIPPIANS 3:12

None of us have got there yet. We are all in a work in progress and sometimes all we can do is *aim* to hold on, even if it all feels out of reach. And this verse also offers a helpful link between today and tomorrow, when we'll be looking at how God holds us.

## Response

In order to hold on to the good things, we need freed-up, empty hands. What are you holding on to as your comfort blanket? Open your hands, palms up, and make a conscious act of yielding afresh to God.

Above all, we need to hold on to God.

Do you see yourself approaching him nervously, daring only to touch the corner of his prayer shawl?

Or are you like Mary meeting the risen Lord Jesus, wanting to cling on to him and never let go?

Jesus welcomes us, however and whenever we come to him. Reach out for him now, and tell him what's on your heart.

For further reflection and worship, listen to 'You're gonna be okay' by Brian and Jenn Johnson.

## Evening reflection: Freefall not downfall

*'Hold on,' the instructor said,*
*as he clicked me into safety.*
*I leaned one way, then another,*
*testing there was no escape,*
*no chance of falling.*
*Ahead of me, the zip-wire*
*snaked across the forest clearing*
*housing a play-park,*
*the children paying no heed*
*to the silly grown-ups whizzing past*
*high above their heads.*
*'Hold on!'*
*No need to hear it twice,*
*no hardship*
*to heed its advice.*
*Fingers clenched, muscles primed,*
*a push of my legs*
*and I was flying.*
*Flying!*
*If I shrieked it was but*
*exhilaration finding voice,*
*not fear;*
*no, most certainly not fear.*
*For my holding on was but a tiny demand*
*when the straps around me*
*gripped me so very tightly.*

# 25

# FINDING STRENGTH THROUGH BEING HELD

> **So do not fear, for I am with you; do not be dismayed, for I am your God. I will strengthen you and help you; I will uphold you with my righteous right hand.**
> ISAIAH 41:10

> **He will cover you with his feathers, and under his wings you will find refuge; his faithfulness will be your shield and rampart.**
> PSALM 91:4

> **For I am the Lord your God who takes hold of your right hand and says to you, Do not fear; I will help you.**
> ISAIAH 41:13

Yesterday we looked at holding on: making a conscious decision to take hold of what is good and to cling on, knowing our lives depend on it. Today we're considering the reverse of that: that God takes hold of us, his good creation, and never lets go, knowing our lives depend on it.

God created much of the universe by his spoken command: '"Let there be light," and there was light' (Genesis 1:3), and so on. But when it comes to creating humankind, the Bible makes it clear how hands-on God was in the process. It's easy to think of the characters in the 'Wallace and Gromit' films, painstakingly fashioned out of modelling clay, with the early versions having the maker's fingerprints clearly visible. As I've said before, I love to think of us having God's fingerprints all over us, don't you?

God is not a God who is strong but distant.

His strength does not need to be imagined or conjured up or, for that matter, reached out for, as if it's too far away.

> **'God did this so that they would seek him and perhaps reach out for him and find him, though he is not far from any one of us.'**
> ACTS 17:27

God is near.

He is within touching distance.

We are held within his embrace.

During the Covid-19 pandemic, the thing that so many of us craved was touch. A wave through a window or a feeble elbow bump simply didn't cut it. There is something so powerful about interpersonal connection when it's expressed physically. And perhaps this is the very thing that causes us problems when thinking of connecting with God to access his loving strength: he isn't flesh and blood, is he? (At least, not physically present in front of us.) How can God connect with our physicality? How can we feel his touch?

The first, easy, answer is that he uses other people. If we have ever been the recipient of a hug intended to demonstrate love and compassion and felt it deep in our soul, or if we have ever had someone take our hand and felt that it's met our every need in that moment, then I believe this is evidence of God at work. The interpersonal takes on something of the supernatural, as God himself invades the space as close to physically as he can.

The second answer is akin to this, in a more satisfying way but one which is perhaps harder to get our heads around: that God, even while being transcendent, can hold us as perfectly as *if* he were flesh. Let me tell you, by way of illustration, about a friend of mine, who has what she calls her 'magic blanket'. Frankly, we need to use a fair bit of imagination there, since it's barely more than an ancient rag now; but if ever I got upset, she would say, 'Time for the magic blanket.' I think it was more to do with her concern than any inherent powers in that threadbare thing, but when she draped it over my shoulders, I felt comforted. Always. Fast forward to today, and I no longer live near that friend, but I still recall the peace of those times, so much so that when I need to sense God's palpable presence, I pray, 'God, I need your magic blanket.' (I realise I may be losing some credibility here, but bear with!) The thing is, whenever I pray that, I sense God covering me, as if with that blanket, and the peace and comfort I crave settle on me. Honestly, it's as close to a physical sensation as you can imagine. It sounds flaky, but it's one of the many, many marvels of God.

Moments like that achieve more than just a dose of peace, a temporary fix. When we have known, felt, or sensed God hold us, it imbues a strength that continues long afterwards. God is never careless in his handling of us. That's such an important truth to grasp. If we have known other people give meaningless physical contact, even leaving us confused as to what and why, then be sure that God never treats us like that. He comes near because he loves us and wants to connect with us; and when God connects, it's with covenantal impact. We may not always sense his presence, and that can be distressing, but he has never withdrawn. He promised to never leave us nor forsake us (Deuteronomy 31:6), and we have to believe that.

Let's move on to consider three ways God holds us. Taking our cue from the first Isaiah verse, we will start with the idea of upholding, or holding up, using an image of building work or renovation. It is not a bad picture, considering how we are all a restoration work in progress.

I remember a *Grand Designs* episode in which the future dream house was nothing more than a shell of roofless stone walls. There was a real chance the walls would fall down, and the first job was to fix an iron frame to them to shore them up and keep them stable. Life can feel like that, sometimes, when so much has been stripped from us that we feel hollowed out and in danger of collapse.

Take a moment to pause, if you need to, and ask God to show you how he is shoring you up, and ask him to let you feel it.

The second way God holds us is in embrace, under his wings, so to speak. When my sons were small and hurt themselves, their tears were hard to bear for both of us. We would wrap our arms around each other, me saying, 'Just hold on until it feels better.' Their grip would become all the tighter at that point, as if to better extract the comfort from me, but then their muscles would relax, the sobbing would ease, and they could face the rest of the day. They were the ones to pull away, when they were ready. Likewise, God never disconnects himself from our embrace. He longs for us to come to him for strength and comfort – it's part of his job – and we can linger for however short or long a time. Unlike a mere human embrace, though, God's hug brings genuine restoration.

Thirdly, God holds us by taking our hand, with the encouragement that we don't need to fear or worry. There are so many different contexts in which an offered hand hits the spot: to express companionship, to stop us losing our balance, to help us over a stile or a puddle, to reassure someone of our presence. In some, there is practical help ('Give us a hand, would you?') while in others the need met is an emotional one. I wonder what our greatest need of God's hand is today? Whatever it is, we can be sure his arm is outstretched, fingers already twitching in anticipation. ('Take my hand, won't you?')

## Response

Spend some time quietly thinking about God holding you. How do you need it to feel – as an embrace, or a covering, or holding you steady?

Ask him to make his presence known – and don't rush away too quickly from it.

*Loving God, thank you for letting me sense your presence. I need you to do a powerful, supernatural work in me. Give me your strength, comfort, and peace; your reassurance and security; and may they last and last, as you do. Amen.*

For further reflection and worship, listen to 'Just be held' by Casting Crowns.

## Evening reflection: The contented child

**I have calmed and quietened myself, I am like a weaned child with its mother; like a weaned child I am content.**
PSALM 131:2

*Not for me the wriggling*
*of a child desperate to be freed*
*from a parent's confining hold.*
*Not for me the shrugging off*
*of an arm laid across my shoulder.*
*Not for me the refusal of God's call*
*to come, just come*
*and be held.*
*No.*
*I am the child content in the embrace,*
*secure in the love,*
*cocooned in the warmth,*
*wanting to be nowhere, ever,*
*but here.*
*There's time enough for tasks tomorrow,*
*their demands already knocking.*
*Here and now is the place and time*
*for soothing*
*and comfort,*
*rest and deep refreshing.*
*I am the child who sleeps on*
*the chest of their Father,*
*held.*

# 26

# FINDING STRENGTH THROUGH REST

> **This is what the Sovereign Lord, the Holy One of Israel, says: 'In repentance and rest is your salvation, in quietness and trust is your strength, but you would have none of it.'**
>
> ISAIAH 30:15

Before we go any further, read the above verse again, slowly. If it's familiar, it is tempting to skim over it, the way we too easily do. Perhaps put your pencil to work: I'm a great fan of underlining and making notes.

What stands out for you?

Which words have the biggest impact?

We are going to spend our time today going through this verse, section by section. We have already seen the importance of getting ourselves away from everything else – people and situations – and seeking out God alone. This verse speaks more detail into what we might expect from those times. Perhaps it will fill in some of the gaps in our understanding of how.

At the time these words were originally spoken, Israel was being attacked by its enemy Assyria, but instead of turning to God for help, they were relying on Egypt. It's tempting to try and draw our strength from sources other than God, and sometimes we barely notice we are doing it. But in response to Israel's situation, God himself speaks through Isaiah.

He is described here as the 'Sovereign Lord, the Holy One'. In other words, he's the one in charge, the one we should acknowledge as supreme. We can insert here our own expressions, to make it personal: he is our faithful God, our eternal Father, Lord of all, and so on. Pause for a moment. Let awareness of his greatness – his strength – settle your heart and mind. Let peace come as you imagine how big he is and how able. Do you sense it?

Being Sovereign Lord entitles him to say what comes next. This isn't a well-meaning friend saying, 'If I were you…' or 'What you want to do is…' This is God, who knows absolutely every detail of our situation inside and out, not just making a suggestion, in a take-it-or-leave-it kind of way, but stating what we must do, simply and unequivocally.

'In repentance and rest is your salvation.' Reading the words 'repentance' and 'salvation' in the same sentence may imply that this is something to do with our conversion. Let's not skip over it, on to the next part, thinking we are past all that. Instead, let's linger. You see, a more accurate translation of 'repentance' here is 'returning'. We can be saved, we can understand and be grateful for all that Jesus won for us on the cross, but still find ourselves veering off course, getting distracted, becoming sidetracked. Let's face it, even in reading this chapter, our minds are wandering! And when that wandering has taken us away from our closeness to God, when our troublesome circumstances have been shouting louder than his word, then our connection with the source of our strength is compromised and even broken.

This is why God urges us to return. If that returning involves fresh repentance, then all the better! But the bottom line is that he wants to help us, to give us what we need, and for that to happen we need to come back to him, to refocus our attention on him. If my experience is anything to go by, we may need to do this multiple times a day.

'In quietness and trust is your strength.' It's another of those great soundbites, but, once again, just saying it to ourselves is not what makes it effective. There's more treasure to unearth if we dig a little deeper. For clarity, in referring to 'quietness' I don't believe God is addressing personality traits here. I don't think God is particularly applauding the introverted or celebrating the shy. It doesn't read to me as one of God's upside-down philosophies, like 'The first shall be last' and 'The meek shall inherit the earth'. Rather, this is a call to all of us to stop our endless mental chatter, with its declared plans and schedules. Our heads don't need to operate like an open-plan office full of All That Noise.

Let's stop.

And breathe.

This doesn't all rely on us.

The Sovereign Lord is in charge…

… which leads seamlessly to 'and trust'.

Whenever we choose to trust God for the outcome, trust that he will answer our prayers, trust he will do what is best, we are consciously taking our hands off the steering wheel and letting him take control. Keep in mind that we're talking about the Sovereign Lord, since he alone is the only one who can be utterly trusted.

Trust takes away all the striving – what happens is not up to us.

Trust not only makes our burdens of responsibility lighter, but completely lifts them from us.

Trust enables us to say, 'Not my will but yours be done.' This is not us adopting a fatalistic or resigned 'qué será, será' ('what will be, will be') attitude, but agreeing with God that he is in charge and will work in our best interests (Romans 8:28). Habakkuk puts it so well:

> **Though the fig-tree does not bud and there are no grapes on the vines, though the olive crop fails and the fields produce no food, though there are no sheep in the sheepfold and no cattle in the stalls, yet I will rejoice in the Lord, I will be joyful in God my Saviour. The Sovereign Lord is my strength; he makes my feet like the feet of a deer, he enables me to tread on the heights.**
> HABAKKUK 3:17–19

In other words, if our prayers aren't answered in the way we hoped, if we see no material change in our situation, or if the people we're praying for show no sign of change, even then, we don't need to be weighed down by it all. We don't have to fear that God is not on our side after all, because we claim the promise of scripture that he is (Psalm 118:6).

Can we dare to whisper: 'Lord, I trust you – even in *this*?'

'But you would have none of it.' Those words could have been addressed directly to me – perhaps you felt that, too? And in the light of our exploration so far, it feels all the more tragic that I can recall all those times when I have squirmed and resisted and positively opposed God's invitation to return and rest, to be quiet and find strength.

When I was first signed off from work with clinical depression, after my father's death, it was a natural instinct – a primal urge almost – to fill the time. I was stressed to breaking point and barely sleeping and yet at first I found myself buzzing from one task to another. It was years later that my therapist told me that overworking, not allowing rest, was in fact a typical trauma response, all of it an elaborate ruse to stop me having to think.

It's tragically common.

It takes a supreme amount of effort to avoid thinking about what threatens to harm us, and yet that very system of avoidance will cause us trouble of its own at some point.

How about we respond to God's patient invitation? (It's not too late; there's no expiry date.)

In repentance and rest is our salvation.

In quietness and trust is our strength.

Let's choose to want all of it.

## Response

This will take some time to process, so make a start today that you can build on.

Jot down in a notebook the things you have been turning to in place of resting in God, and lay them before him.

If you are ready to, repent and turn back to him. You may find acting this out with physical movements helpful.

Pledge to do differently, with God's help.

Affirm your intention by spending a few minutes in complete silence, breathing deeply to aid resting, then turn your thoughts into prayers.

For further reflection and worship, listen to 'Come to Jesus (Rest in him)' by Keith and Kristyn Getty.

## Evening reflection: Be still, my soul

*God, I've done it again:*
*failed to follow the creator's instructions.*
*In my eagerness –*
*no, make that wilful, blind determination –*
*to get on with the job,*
*I've shrugged you off.*
*As in a marathon,*
*you were offering water from the sidelines,*
*but I limped past,*
*ignoring the gesture,*
*missing that you were there to help.*
*Why do I do it?*
*I mean, why do I still do it,*
*when I know the theory?*
*How come I arrive at the end of the day*
*so spent,*
*so depleted?*
*'Arise, my love, my beautiful one, and come away'**
*says the lover to his beloved.*
*'Come with me by yourselves to a quiet place and get some rest'***
*says Jesus to his disciples.*
*Can I hear those words cutting through the striving?*
*Can it be true that you're saying them to me, Lord?*
*Yes, my heart knows it to be so.*
*Scoop me up, Lord, hold me close.*
*Let me rest.*

*Song of Songs 2:10 (ESV)
**Mark 6:31

# 27

# FINDING STRENGTH THROUGH PRAISING GOD

> **Shout for joy to God, all the earth! Sing the glory of his name; make his praise glorious. Say to God, 'How awesome are your deeds! So great is your power that your enemies cringe before you. All the earth bows down to you; they sing praise to you, they sing the praises of your name.'**
> PSALM 66:1–4

We're thinking today about the importance of praising God as a means of finding 'strength in the Lord' (1 Samuel 30:6). Knowing that this phrase originated with David, who was a prolific writer of praise songs that went on to be recorded in the book of Psalms, it's safe to assume that this was a key way that he did so.

I remember many years ago reading the book *Power in Praise* by Merlin Carothers. It took as its premise Paul's exhortation to 'give thanks in all circumstances; for this is God's will for you in Christ Jesus' (1 Thessalonians 5:18). Actually, Carothers went further, advocating that we give thanks *for* all circumstances, giving testimony after testimony of the miracles born from such prayers. As we shall see today, there is great benefit in praising God, but I have to issue a warning: let's be sure our motives are right. The danger is that our praise will be not so much driven by awe at God's greatness, but by what results we might get. So, let's not be treating it as a kind of heavenly slot machine!

When we're going through troubles of any kind, they are often all-consuming. They have a magnetic mental pull that's incredibly difficult to resist. If we manage to get distracted for a while, we might find that we've forgotten about 'it', but the moment it comes back to mind, we're sucked in by it all over again. The Bible, meanwhile, is filled with encouragement for us to look up, to focus on God, to consciously think of other things. For example:

> **My soul is downcast within me; therefore I will remember you from the land of the Jordan, the heights of Hermon – from Mount Mizar.**
> PSALM 42:6

When we turn our gaze intentionally towards our lovely God, the things we are anxious about start to fade into the background and our hearts are freed to fill once more with love which we express through praise and worship. A friend said to me recently, 'If your problems seem bigger than your God, you've really got a problem.' One of the reasons praising God is so effective and beneficial is that it recalibrates our perspective. The writers of the psalms testify to the fact that when we praise God because he is worthy, we find our burdens lifted, our strength returning. Little, if anything, has changed in the situation itself, but within our hearts everything feels improved.

Of course, this is easier said than done. How are we supposed to praise when we feel 'meh'? Surely God wants heartfelt devotion, not our tear-stained mumblings?

The key, I think, is in that word 'heartfelt'. God understands how our hearts feel and wants us to come to him on bad days as well as good. The psalms demonstrate well this honest approach, so let's work our way through one to learn how it's done. I've chosen Psalm 64, because of how it starts:

> **Hear me, my God, as I voice my complaint; protect my life from the threat of the enemy.**
> PSALM 64:1

This is no polite, trite introduction. Rather, it feels like David has grabbed God by the lapels in his desperation to be heard. He blurts out what his enemy is like: 'sharpen[ing] their tongues like swords and aim[ing] cruel words like deadly arrows' (v. 3). There is no 'I know these are your children, God, and I'm sorry for being so…' This is the power of honesty: no second-guessing, no filter, no twisting ourselves in knots over the theology; just stating the miserable, terrifying facts as we see them. It doesn't sound like praise yet, but already by verse 7 a shift is occurring: 'But God will shoot them with his arrows; they will suddenly be struck down.'

This is where our honesty takes us: in addressing God about the things that bother us, we are looking him in the face. It's not long before his face – ever-kind, ever-welcoming – becomes our focus. The burden has been blurted out and has not so much been laid down as fallen from our grip. The thought comes to us: God can sort this out! He can mess with my enemies better than they've messed with me. He's bigger! He's greater! He's on my side! And soon everyone will see it, as laid out in verse 9: 'All people will fear; they will proclaim the works of God and ponder what he has done.'

At this point, we may find we're doing our own pondering. Memories start to pop up of times we've prayed before, times God has come through before. Something is stirring inside – could it be hope? It's certainly the start of praise. We weren't in the mood when we started but, goodness, God is so wonderful and I have to let him know!

David's praises lifted his eyes to the God he loved and demonstrated the truth of Isaiah 26:3: 'You will keep in perfect peace those whose minds are steadfast, because they trust in you.' This isn't about coming away from a time of praise with a greater sense of resilience but with the blessing of God's strength through connecting with him.

The closing verse of Psalm 64 declares: 'The righteous will rejoice in the Lord and take refuge in him; all the upright in heart will glory in him!' I think David stopped there just so he could lay his pen to one side and worship. Do you sense that, even now, as we read it?

Strength came to David from this type of encounter with God, and it can potentially do so from every praise time for us. We don't have to be in a formal setting, with musicians and set words. We can be on our own, doing whatever feels comfortable for us, following this kind of pattern:

1 We come as we are, however upset or anxious or burdened.
2 Turning our eyes towards Jesus, we look away from what is bothering us so our perspective is reset and our thinking realigned with God's word.
3 Letting go of all the 'stuff' and reaching out for God encourages a deep connection with him.
4 Laying ourselves bare before him, we can be confident of his acceptance.
5 We're reminding ourselves of his goodness and every other virtue. Through words written by others, enhanced by what our own hearts express, we're declaring again how great our God is.
6 The Holy Spirit brings to mind the times in the past when we've seen God work and releases thanksgiving and gratitude.
7 This, in turn, stirs our faith for him to do it again, leading to…
8 Hope, which leads us to…
9 Worship.

We may not always feel like praising God but, believe me, he is always worthy of it.

We can choose to worship.

Let's do so.

## Response

Before doing anything too formal, spend a few moments praising and thanking God in your own words, singing a song if you want to – although wonder can be expressed in silence, too.

How about trying to write your own psalm? It doesn't have to be well-crafted or fancy, but it does need to be honest. Write down whatever you want to say to God today. Start with the first thing you need to blurt out, then be open to where that leads you. Keep your focus on him and let him draw you nearer to his throne, where praise and worship can tumble out.

How about singing your own song? Start with a line that you can repeat as many times as you like, then see how it develops. You might be surprised at what you hear yourself singing.

For further reflection and worship, listen to 'Praise' by Elevation Worship.

## Evening reflection: Turn your eyes upon Jesus

**Turn your eyes upon Jesus, look full in his wonderful face; and the things of earth will grow strangely dim, in the light of his glory and grace.**
Helen Howarth Lemmel, 1922

*Oh, the sweetness of a familiar song,*
*each line of tune fresh*
*in my mind and on my lips,*
*as it ever was.*
*And its truth burns like a beacon*
*lighting the way for me*
*and all God's followers.*
*'Turn your eyes upon Jesus' –*
*yes, and a thousand times yes.*
*Your face, Lord, is all I seek.*
*Your name lifts my heart at its sound.*
*Jesus, precious Jesus,*
*let the things that have plagued me today,*
*robbing me of joy,*
*sapping my strength,*
*fade as surely as the daylight has now.*
*Let all else be eclipsed by your glory.*
*Here, I lay all my troubles at your feet,*
*before lying down to sleep –*
*in peace and security because Jesus is Lord.*
*Yes, Jesus is Lord.*

# 28

# FINDING STRENGTH IN JOY

**'This day is holy to the Lord your God. Do not mourn or weep.' For all the people had been weeping as they listened to the words of the Law. Nehemiah said, 'Go and enjoy choice food and sweet drinks, and send some to those who have nothing prepared. This day is holy to our Lord. Do not grieve, for the joy of the Lord is your strength.' The Levites calmed all the people, saying, 'Be still, for this is a holy day. Do not grieve.'**
NEHEMIAH 8:9–11

**Weeping may stay for the night, but rejoicing comes in the morning.**
PSALM 30:5

When life becomes painful or difficult, joy is often the first thing to leave, and its absence saps our energy. With everyone wearing their masks so successfully around us, we may be left concluding that happiness is only for other people, not for us. Putting on a brave front or trying to make light of it only proves that we can't strive or force our way into joy. The good news for our weary souls is that joy is a God-given gift.

In Sunday school I was told that joy stood for Jesus-Others-Yourself. Putting ourselves squarely at the bottom of the heap was the way to lasting contentment, or so I heard it. It's true that serving Jesus and caring for other people brings satisfaction, but I question whether it's the actual source of real happiness. On the other hand, our current self-obsessed, me-me-me culture, where we place ourselves teeteringly high on top of the heap, might bring moments of fun and enjoyment, but it's still not real joy.

I once knew a lady called Phoebe (a fitting name, meaning 'bright, shining') who had recently become a Christian. She radiated happiness, lighting up every room with her smiling presence. She told everyone she met about Jesus and what a difference he had made. (Not that she needed to, since it was so obvious.) But then, after a special celebratory meal with the family, Phoebe's only daughter decided not to go home with her parents but to drive over to a friend's to stay the night. Tragically, she fell asleep at the wheel and drove into a wall, being killed instantly.

As the whole church tried to process the enormous shock, I remember wondering what would happen to Phoebe now. Her faith was so new. Surely this would completely derail her. The funeral was one of those horribly incongruent types: the church filled with vibrant young adults whose lives lay ahead of them, while one of their number lay in a coffin. Everyone was in tears, as you would expect, but even through the tears Phoebe's smile was still there. Her joy amid the tragedy felt nothing short of miraculous. It was a gift to all of us.

In that season, and for the years following, Phoebe demonstrated something powerful wherever she went: that joy had little to do with life's circumstances, but everything to do with God at work. I have heard some people say that joy is a deep-down thing, while happiness is more superficial. But true joy, that is indeed rooted deeply within us, will keep bursting through to the surface. It reminds me of those wild flowers (alright, weeds) that somehow manage to grow through tarmac and concrete – their inherent life-giving energy is dynamic and unstoppable. In the case of joy, that irrepressible lifeforce stems from it being part of the character of God himself.

In Galatians 5, the apostle Paul lists what he calls the 'fruit of the Spirit': 'love, joy, peace, forbearance, kindness, goodness, faithfulness, gentleness, and self-control' (vv. 22–23). The Holy Spirit represents the very essence of God, so this fruit is describing elements of his nature. We can therefore say God is love, God is joy, God is peace, and so on, and each attribute would be a perfect fit. Aquinas put it this way:

> God is happiness by his essence: for he is happy not by acquisition or participation of something else, but by his essence.

Since we are created in God's image, it follows that we have a capacity for joy and happiness within us, simply by virtue of being alive. And where this joy has been squashed and squeezed, trampled and trashed, we can receive fresh filling through the Holy Spirit.

Do you hear this?

We have not 'lost our sense of humour'.

We are not unable to see 'the funny side'.

Or, even if that is so, it is completely understandable why. We have been hurt and damaged, our confidence is diminished, our hope even more so. Yet joy can be ours, and it is found in God, as Augustine declares:

> Following after God is the desire of happiness; to reach God is happiness itself.

It's an astonishing truth that joy can be present where there are no real reasons for happiness. Whenever we experience a 'joy that passes understanding' (to misquote a phrase) in situations that don't warrant it, it's not because we are denying our loss or grief or whatever. As Professor Lindsey Godwin observes:

> The answer I've come to embrace is this: joy isn't just allowed – it's necessary. In a world that can feel overwhelming and heartbreaking, moments of laughter, play, or connection aren't a betrayal of reality.[10]

Let's pause there for a moment. Some of us haven't found life funny for a very long time. Some can't remember the last time we laughed, or even felt like smiling. If joy is like light coming into darkness, we can't seem to find the light switch. It may provide another opportunity for lament, for grieving over this lack of joy. We miss that side of us and are wistful about its return.

Take hope.

God wants to do what Isaiah promised:

> **'Forget the former things; do not dwell on the past. See, I am doing a new thing! Now it springs up; do you not perceive it? I am making a way in the wilderness and streams in the wasteland.'**
> ISAIAH 43:18–19

The context of the Nehemiah verses quoted at the start of this chapter is that Jerusalem's city walls have now been completely rebuilt. It was a tough project, met with all kinds of opposition, but the workers had rallied together and seen it through. Now, the law is being read to the people and they are cut to the quick by its message. They are heartbroken and dismayed, yet Nehemiah urges them not to see it like that. God is with them, there is no need to grieve – 'The joy of the Lord is [our] strength.'

Joy acts like fuel for our souls. It burns within us like a tiny pilot light, ready to burst into flame, even when there seems no reason to be joyful.

Life, meanwhile, conspires to suck the joy out of us, to dampen that spark. Sometimes the battle rages hard, 24/7, and in our despair we cry ourselves to sleep. Psalm 30:5 is a verse to cling to: that even the most tear-stained night can witness joy returning in the morning. Even though nothing may have changed, God is still with us, still the giver of joy.

> **The light shines in the darkness, and the darkness has not overcome it.**
> JOHN 1:5

## Response

There are several different ways of taking this forward. Joy isn't all about fun and laughter, but even smiling can lift our spirits and kick-start change on the inside.

1 Do something that makes you laugh: watch a TV show, tell an old joke, or meet a friend. Exercise that funny muscle!
2 Make a gratitude list, thanking God for as many good things as you can think of.
3 Make a list of 'joy thieves', those things that steal your joy, then offer them to God.
4 Last but definitely not least: pray for a fresh infilling of the Holy Spirit, to replenish your joy tank.

For further reflection and worship, listen to 'Joy of the Lord' by Rend Collective.

## Evening reflection: Unaccustomed joy

*I made myself laugh today,*
*my cheek muscles almost snapping in shock.*
*It wasn't even funny,*
*not really,*
*just one of those silly things*
*that catch your eye*
*and tickle your funny bone.*
*Oh, how I thanked God*
*for the relief of it,*
*a reminder of old times*
*when life wasn't so…*
*serious,*
*all-consuming,*
*tough.*
*The child within burst from the wings,*
*unhid from the curtain,*
*rushing on to the stage,*
*where she twirled in sweet abandon,*
*the limelight glancing off her hair.*
*This picture of joy I shall carry*
*when the darkness falls again,*
*as I know it will.*
*Somewhere, deep inside,*
*a part of me knows a better truth:*
*there is treasure, precious treasure*
*being mined,*
*being mine.*

# 29
# THE RELIEF OF KNOWING OUR LIMITS

> **'Can you bind the chains of the Pleiades? Can you loosen Orion's belt? Can you bring forth the constellations in their seasons or lead out the Bear with its cubs? Do you know the laws of the heavens? Can you set up God's dominion over the earth?'**
> JOB 38:31–33

> **There is a time for everything, and a season for every activity under the heavens: a time to be born and a time to die.**
> ECCLESIASTES 3:1–2

'I'm doing too much,' I declared to a lovely Christian friend some years ago. 'What do you think I should let go of?' She is a wise woman, and I expected her to relay some sweet godly advice. Instead, she batted it away. 'Nah, you're young yet. Do it all!'

It didn't help.

Today we're looking at limits and boundaries, and what a blessing they are in a world that constantly pushes us to exceed them. Feeling tired? Take this energy drink and carry on as normal. Can't afford what you want? Take this line of credit. The list goes on, with its encouragement to disregard any signs of weakness because We Are Strong. The propaganda message is a clear one: limitations are there to be overridden or ignored. The truth, however, is that only God is limitless, and those boundaries he has created within and around us are for our benefit.

The verses from Job might seem strange ones to look at. They come from the closing chapters of the book, following the story of how

Job – a righteous man of God – was chosen by Satan to be the object of an experiment: throw as much suffering at him and watch what happens to his faith. We hear a lot *about* God through the course of the book, his 'friends' being generous in their opinions as to why this is all going on. Meanwhile, Job longs for God himself, for the relationship they used to enjoy and the blessings of that intimacy. Finally, God shows up and, in his inimitable way, has the final word.

Take time to read Job 38—41 and you will find a masterclass of God revealing how awesome he truly is. The world is described as a vast, unfathomable place, created by God and filled with huge creatures that could knock a person sideways with a flap of their eyelashes. 'Can you do that?' God asks Job. Of course not, and Job's only response is to admit:

> **'I know that you can do all things; no purpose of yours can be thwarted. You asked, "Who is this that obscures my plans without knowledge?" Surely I spoke of things I did not understand, things too wonderful for me to know.'**
> JOB 42:1–3

The bottom line is this: humans are finite beings, with physical, mental, and spiritual limits. Hollywood would have us flying, running up walls, or becoming invisible. The harsh reality is that although we can dream the impossible dream, there is only so much we can actually do. And far from clipping our wings and spoiling our fun, this message is not only a positive one in its own right, but one which can set us free.

At a speed awareness course (don't judge!), I listened to the attendees' stories of how they came to be there. One chap worked in management for a supermarket chain, and he regularly travelled from store to store. Although he had been caught this time doing 86 mph, he confessed to me in the coffee break that he had once done 120 mph in the course of his work. It made my 56 mph, entering a 50 mph section of roadworks, seem tame. I couldn't fathom the lightning-quick reactions he would have needed at that speed: split seconds to make decisions that could make the difference between life and death. And all so that he could meet his boss' unrealistic expectations.

How often have we felt under pressure to do something that we wouldn't have chosen to, or pressure to exceed our natural limits?

How many times have we ended up saying 'yes', when we'd been so determined not to?

Wouldn't it be wonderful to have the freedom to say and do what we actually wanted?

Meanwhile, the pressures come from all sides. Even a simple trip to the shops is a battle to resist the products they entice us to buy. We might hope that being in church offers shelter from it all, but often it's the place where the pressure is most intense. Why? Perhaps because of approaches like: 'I really sense you'd be great at the children's work. You seem to have a natural gift there. How about coming along to the meeting on Thursday evening, and we'll get you signed up?' In smaller churches, people can easily end up on several teams just to keep the programme going. How do we say 'no' when there's no one else to do it? And it's not as if we want to just be attendees ('pew-fillers', as we used to call them). We may not even recognise it as pressure at the time, so keen are we for God to use us, but it's an area that requires a lot of wisdom.

Let's look at something Jesus said, in his prayer to his Father:

> **'I have brought you glory on earth by finishing the work you gave me to do.'**
> JOHN 17:4

This is what the evangelist J. John said about this verse when addressing the Christian Resources Together retreat in 2018:

> Did he [finish the work]? Did he really? Surely there were many more people he could have healed; many more he could have brought to know the truth? There was so much more he could have done. The Lord could have started when he was 18 (like most YWAMers!) If he had, he could have had more years in ministry and left the church in better shape when he "went up". But, if you consider that his job was to die on a cross and to rise from the dead in order to give us redemption, deliverance and salvation, then Jesus did complete the work the Father gave him to do.
>
> The thing to realise is that God doesn't expect us to do everything. Many of us in ministry have got so many irons in the fire we've actually put the fire out. Here's a motto that's worth repeating: 'If your output exceeds your input, then your upkeep will be your downfall.'

The key factor for Jesus is that he knew what he had come to Earth to do. Remember when a desperate father pleaded with Jesus to come with him *now* because his daughter was dying (Luke 8:42)? He didn't go, at least not straightaway. It wasn't out of selfishness or ignorance or because he couldn't be bothered. It was because his clear-minded focus was on bringing glory to God. Everything was chosen or discarded according to that unequivocal mission.

Some of us know we are living beyond our limits.

What we've called our 'busy/trying season' has itself felt limitless.

How about, instead of feeling weak and useless over having to say, 'I can't do it', we learn to recognise this pressure to perform as yet another burden to be laid down?

We are safe having limited resources and limited capacity, because we are in the hands of an almighty, limitless God who is waiting to pour everything we need into us.

He loves us without limit.

There is nowhere too far away for him to reach us.

He neither slumbers nor sleeps.

This is our God!

## Response

If you have an elastic band to hand, slowly stretch it out as far as it will go. You know that if you over-stretch it, it will snap and likely sting you.

Let God speak to you about the ways you have been over-extending yourself.

Ask him for the strength to say no.

Thank him for caring about every detail of your life and how you live it.

For further reflection and worship, listen to 'You say' by Lauren Daigle.

## Evening reflection: All praise to mighty God!

*God, you are mighty,*
*altogether able,*
*eternally present,*
*your love and faithfulness enduring*
*through each generation.*
*Your grace and mercy course not only through my veins*
*but through the whole of history.*
*How I need this reminder of your greatness*
*in contrast to my perfectly crafted puniness!*
*My efforts are too often*
*focused on overcoming my humanity*
*when all that is required*
*is to rest in your divinity.*
*My body and mind are tired, Lord,*
*and sleep is calling my name.*
*Let me cast all my worrisome burdens*
*on you, my mighty, altogether able God.*
*All glory to you,*
*all thanks and praise,*
*Forever and ever!*

# 30

# GO IN THE STRENGTH YOU HAVE

**The Lord turned to him and said, 'Go in the strength you have and save Israel out of Midian's hand. Am I not sending you?'**
JUDGES 6:14

**'How many loaves do you have?' he asked. 'Go and see.' When they found out, they said, 'Five – and two fish.'**
MARK 6:38

We're looking today at a verse that acts as a motto, as we consider moving forward: 'Go in the strength you have.' That applies even if we think our strength is pathetically small! Before David defeated Goliath using just a pebble fired from a sling, the people around him tried to set him up with Saul's armour (1 Samuel 17:38–39). It was huge on him, and didn't so much arm him as swamp him. It's a great picture of trying to fit someone else's image of what strong looks like. The fact is, we only need to look at ourselves in the mirror to find the answer to the question of what strength looks like: coming to God as we are, and watching what he does with us.

In reading the Bible, we don't find many examples of great things being achieved with great resources; in fact, it's pretty much the opposite. And this is the curious thing about the God we love and serve: he simply doesn't view things or operate the way we do.

He doesn't see time in the same way.

Nor weakness or strength.

He doesn't see mountains as obstacles.

Yet the fact that God has ways that are not our ways is not something that separates us from him; rather it acts as an invitation to come over to his side and do things his way.

Our starting point is something like this: 'God, I'm growing daily but I'm still weak. I want to learn how to do what you do. Show me what I'm missing here!'

So, let's literally start small. As small as a seed, in fact. Back in the days I used to garden, I can't remember which kind of seed it was, but I wished I'd not been trying to sow on such a windy day. Those things were like dust and bore no relation to the picture on the front of the packet. How can it possibly be that a huge plant, or even a tree, can develop from such tiny origins? I think God has great fun messing with our heads like that! How can…? But…? And God just smiles and says, 'Watch and see!'

Perhaps the strength you've been seeking God for is like a seed. It might be tiny, nestled deep within you, not quite breaking the surface and making itself visible, but it is there nonetheless. Ask that speck of dust 'What strength do you have?' and its answer would be: 'Within me is the power and potential for the life of a beautiful, flowering, fruiting plant.'

Do you get that?

The seed looks nothing like its parent plant, and yet it's kind of the same.

Take that further with us actually being made in the image of God. Ask ourselves, 'What strength do you have?' and our answer could be: 'Within me is all the power and potential from God for a flourishing life.'

It might feel too much of a stretch, yet this is the essence of everything we've looked at so far. It doesn't depend on us. God's narrative about our human finiteness is different from the one we have so far been listening to. It's a new day.

Let's look at the two stories highlighted in today's verses. We read about Gideon in the book of Judges, who were the God-appointed rulers in the period before Israel had a monarchy. Among their ranks is Deborah, a mighty warrior, fearless against the enemy, and Samson, the fabled strong man, albeit with a fatal flaw, who finally made things right before God by giving up his life. The word we would use for them is 'hero'. Not so with Gideon. Frankly, he comes over as a bit of a wuss, and when an angel of the Lord came to commission him, he was threshing wheat indoors in a wine press, hiding from the enemy. I'm being unfair, of course. He had good reason to be scared of the Midianites, whose strategy was to raid Israelite territory, repeatedly stripping the land of crops and assets. If Gideon had managed to finally harvest some wheat, there was no way he'd leave it vulnerable.

When the angel arrived, he greeted Gideon, 'The Lord is with you, mighty warrior' (Judges 6:12). I imagine him turning around to see who the warrior was behind him. But this message comes from God, the one who 'calls into being things that were not' (Romans 4:17). It's like us greeting an acorn, 'Greetings, mighty oak tree.' God could see in Gideon what others and he himself could not: God's almighty power, God's awesome strength.

When Gideon had finished his terrified blubbering, the angel spoke: 'Go in the strength you have and save Israel out of Midian's hand. Am I not sending you?' I suspect God intended it to be the final word here, but Gideon hadn't finished being terrified. (I love Gideon. Don't you?!)

'Pardon me, my lord,' Gideon replied, 'but how can I save Israel? My clan is the weakest in Manasseh, and I am the least in my family' (Judges 6:15). I imagine his words coming out in a stutter, 'P-p-pardon...' He was overwhelmed and this commission was making no sense. Then came the reply, which didn't end the conversation but at least settled the 'how': 'I will be with you' (v. 16).

This, truly, is the 'secret' to going out in strength: the presence of God with us the entire time. You may remember a conversation Moses had with God regarding their progress into the promised land: 'If your Presence does not go with us, do not send us up from here' (Exodus 33:15). It would make a great daily prayer for each of us.

As the story unfolds, we read of the resounding victory God brought about through 300 soldiers bearing only trumpets, empty jars, and torches. They didn't even need to fight, since their enemy turned on itself. This is the mystery and marvel of doing things God's way. It makes no logical sense, and yet we cannot deny what happens when we obey his directions.

Our second story, the feeding of the 5,000, shows another aspect of the same lesson. A boy's packed lunch is a laughably small amount to share among so many hungry people; no, make that an impossibly small amount. God, though, is in the business of making all things possible, and this pathetic food, offered sacrificially by the boy (who risked staying hungry) and offered again to God with thanksgiving by Jesus, not only went the distance, but several laps more.

Our God is in the multiplication business.

It's never really about what is in our hand, so to speak, but all about what God can do with it once it's yielded. When we bring our honest, puny strength to God, he does extraordinary things with it.

Go in the strength you have, because it is enough – because he is everything.

## Response

Take a garden seed (if you don't have one handy, take a grain of rice), and place it in your palm. What is there within you that feels this small? Is it your faith? Your ability to believe all God has said and done? Or is it your strength that feels miniscule?

Tell God about it, asking him to show you how he sees it.

Then pray, using these words if it helps:

*Almighty God, creator and sustainer of the universe, I thank you for your greatness. Thank you that you are always present with me and there is nothing that's impossible for you. Forgive me for trying to do things in my own strength. Help me place myself in your hands and watch what miracles you will do. Amen.*

For further reflection and worship, listen to 'Christ is enough' by Hillsong Worship.

## Evening reflection: What do you see?

*'What's that in your hand?'*
*His voice came low, inviting.*
*I looked, then looked again*
*and muttered my reply:*
*'It's nothing, just a speck,*
*hardly worth mentioning...'*
*The rush of shame rang in my head.*
*How can I even think of serving*
*the living God*
*with so very, very little?*
*His voice again, cutting through the chaos,*
*Look again.*
*What's in your hand?'*
*I uncurled my palm,*
*eyes tightly shut*
*against the proof for which*
*no reminder was needed.*
*But, aware his gaze was on me,*
*I opened my eyes and gasped.*
*This was a speck no more,*
*but molten lava forcing its way*
*through the splitting side of a volcano.*
*Its fierce and fiery course*
*engulfing the landscape,*
*lighting up earth and sky.*
*'Do you see now?'*
*His voice tender, not rebuking.*
*And I could only bow my head*
*not in shame*
*but in wonder.*

# 31
# TIME TO REFLECT

> **For our light and momentary troubles are achieving for us an eternal glory that far outweighs them all.**
> 2 CORINTHIANS 4:17

> **And we boast in the hope of the glory of God. Not only so, but we also glory in our sufferings, because we know that suffering produces perseverance; perseverance, character; and character, hope.**
> ROMANS 5:2–4

It's our final day together and time for a few more thoughts before we go our separate ways. How grateful we can be for all God has shown us, how he has helped us now and promises to continue in the future.

The aim was never to get ourselves 'all strengthened up' so that we could breeze through the rest of life relying on our increased competence. Instead, the abiding message is how much we need God, in every hour and for everything, and how the strength he offers us depends on us staying connected with him.

It's a reasonable question to ask why we have to go through hardship at all. Isn't there another way of learning the same lessons? I think, as a parent, about how many times I would do anything, *anything at all*, to help my children or spare them pain. Their disappointment, knockbacks, struggles, and heartache are unbearable to witness. If I feel like that, then how come God lets us go through All This?

I heard only recently something I didn't know. When a chick starts to peck through its eggshell, you absolutely mustn't try to help. It might seem a kindness to spare it the effort, but the result will be the death of the chick. You see, all that pecking builds up the strength it needs to survive. So, put bluntly, much as we might dream of an easier life, it's better for us the way it is, with one significant qualification – that we live it God's way.

Pain and suffering are never on our wishlist, but I can tell you a surprising truth: I don't regret what I have had to go through. There are some elements to my story that I hate and want to hide, but still I can say I am glad to have had (almost) all the experiences. Each trial, setback, loss, relationship breakdown, and bereavement has made me hunker more deeply into God, enabling me to discover the Bible's freedom-giving truths more powerfully. I have known the astonishment of hearing God's voice as good as audibly, and receiving those words as the life-belt they were intended to be. I have fought countless battles and somehow remained standing. All because he loves me so.

But it's not just for our own benefit that we go through 'trials of many kinds' (James 1:2). When I became clinically depressed, I remember being consciously grateful for the way it enabled me to empathise with other sufferers. As Paul puts it:

> **Praise be to the God and Father of our Lord Jesus Christ, the Father of compassion and the God of all comfort, who comforts us in all our troubles, so that we can comfort those in any trouble with the comfort we ourselves receive from God.**
> 2 CORINTHIANS 1:3–4

What a source of strength it is to hold each other's hands, to have each other's backs, and to be able to say: 'I know some of what you feel.' It helped redeem my own suffering, to know it would serve others well in the future.

I have repeatedly encouraged us to be honest with ourselves, with others, and with God. I hope that doing so has already proved helpful. It's no good bottling anything up, ever. That's not to say that we pour our hearts out to all and sundry; we need to be wise about who we choose to confide in. The key thing, though, is that burying our pain, disappointment, despair, and so on might put it out of mind, but it doesn't make it go away. The problem simply sinks to a deeper level, where it can fester and become 'infected', leading to depression, bitterness, and other nasties. We shouldn't be surprised, either, if our bodies start to show symptoms rooted in all that repression. Pain needs an outlet – and the best place to express it is at the foot of the cross of Jesus Christ.

This is where our strength lies: not in toughing it out, working on our resilience, thickening our skin, increasing our resolve, but in surrender and letting go. We can daily repeat our commitment: 'Here I am. Take me, use me for my ultimate good, for the benefit of others, and for your glory, Lord.' With this attitude of heart, this willingness to lay down our own requirements, weakness is no longer something to be feared or avoided, but welcomed and embraced. In creating us to be dependent on him – 'weak', if you must – we have an open invitation to connect to the power source that is God himself.

Without him, we can do nothing.

With him, everything is possible.

Joni Eareckson Tada, whose story we heard about in chapter 9, says:

> Perhaps the greatest good that suffering can work for a believer is to increase his or her capacity for God. The greater one's need, the greater will be our capacity, and the greater our capacity, the greater will be our experience of our Saviour.[11]

Joni remains in a wheelchair, despite Jesus being her Saviour and Lord and the one she relies on for daily strength. Many of us will likewise continue to bear outward signs of our weaknesses. Has it ever struck you that when the risen Jesus appeared to his disciples, he still bore the scars from the crucifixion? Wouldn't you think his triumph would be displayed in an unmarked, perfect body? Instead, he modelled what glory can truly look like: when our scars testify to a greater work that

God has done in us. How else can we show others God's strength in us, than with the reminders of what he has brought us through?

One final thought in closing. The Bible makes clear that this kingdom-of-God life is a topsy-turvy one: with the last being first and the meek inheriting the earth. The fact is that the strongest person we could possibly imagine is a puny weakling in God's sight, and the humblest, neediest person can demonstrate a strength that defies description. We've already (in chapter 17) heard from the apostle Paul: 'But God chose the foolish things of the world to shame the wise; God chose the weak things of the world to shame the strong' (1 Corinthians 1:27). He spoke from the experience of feeling like he was the worst of all sinners for the way he persecuted the first Christians, hounding them to death. He knew first-hand what folly his 'wisdom' had proved to be, and had learned through bitter lessons how necessary it was to suffer for God's sake, if he wanted to avail himself of his blessings. It is therefore fitting to finish with Paul's words:

> **But he said to me, 'My grace is sufficient for you, for my power is made perfect in weakness.' Therefore I will boast all the more gladly about my weaknesses, so that Christ's power may rest on me.**
> 2 CORINTHIANS 12:9

James urging us to consider all our trials as 'pure joy' (James 1:2) and Paul telling us he can boast in his weakness might feel a step too far. But what if we tried it God's way?

It's got to be worth a go.

## Response

If you've been keeping notes during the past month, review them and thank God for how far he's brought you. Pray these words, as a pledge to continue:

*Loving God, thank you for your unending covenant with me. I recommit myself to you, that I would seek you every day and let you have your way in me. I give you my weakness and gladly receive your strength. Amen.*

For further reflection and worship, listen to '10,000 reasons (Bless the Lord)' by Matt Redman.

## Evening reflection: He has the final word

*Could there be another way,*
*a different path to take?*
*One that led through peaceful meadows*
*fed by stream and lake*
*and offering refreshment*
*to my weary soul?*

*Might I try another lesson,*
*sit a different test?*
*One that didn't pull and stretch*
*me when I only wanted rest*
*from all life's constant struggles*
*taking their grim toll?*

*'Give me strength!' the frequent cry*
*I uttered night and day;*
*and God was gracious to reply,*
*'I'm all you need in every way;*
*just come to me, my dear one,*
*I can make you whole.*

*'I'm here when the road's so hard*
*you're tempted to give up.*
*I gave you Jesus as the one*
*who drank from the suff'ring-filled cup*
*and took your sin and weakness*
*to ever save your soul.'*

# SECTION III

# Group studies

# GROUP STUDIES OVERVIEW

The following studies offer the opportunity for group discussion around some of the central themes of *Give Me Strength!* The material can be used either independently or alongside the relevant chapters. The given questions are starting points for deeper discussion, with the hope that group members may gain confidence to share and contribute more widely as the weeks unfold. Telling each other our stories is a powerful way of communicating God's work in our lives, in conjunction with the examples and teaching of the Bible.

It's not necessary to have the same leader for each session, but it is important that they spend time in prayerful preparation with the material as well as the relevant chapters of the book. Their role in the group is to facilitate an open, trusting environment in which every attendee feels safe and confident in sharing. They will ensure that no one dominates the meeting and that everyone who wishes to contribute feels their voice is heard – and those who feel they cannot have their silence respected. A simple way of engaging the whole group is to invite attendees to read the Bible passages. The seven group study sessions are as follows:

**Session 1** Let's be honest: we are all weak

**Session 2** Learning from Naomi about regret, grief, and disappointment

**Session 3** Learning from Elijah about burn-out and isolation

**Session 4** God is our refuge and is strong, through and through

**Session 5** How to strengthen ourselves in the Lord: learning from David

**Session 6** The prime importance of connection

**Session 7** Final thoughts

## Session 1

# LET'S BE HONEST: WE ARE ALL WEAK

*Ask attendees to, if possible, read chapters 1 and 2 in advance.*

The sessions and their content are centred on God, the giver of strength. The Bible is full of stories of people who faced all kinds of challenges and overcame them by tapping into God's strength: seeking his wisdom, receiving his goodness, and following his way ahead. However, before we can begin to consider receiving and accessing strength, we must look at what it is to *need* God's strength. In other words, what it means to be weak.

**Ice-breaker questions:** What's the last mistake you made? How easy is it to admit to it?

If you've ever seen a nature programme, or been out in the wild, you will know that nature's motto is 'survival of the fittest'. Strength is displayed by the hunter getting their prey, while the weak are the ones that get picked off. It's not only weak versus strong, but superior versus inferior. We see that same mentality played out in society. Instead of people simply being different from one another, it becomes a case of who's on top and who are the underdogs. Most sadly of all, this temptation to compare ourselves with others happens even in church.

- What kinds of things does our society consider weak?
- Do all of them come with a sense of inferiority?

Thankfully, God does not see things the same way that our culture does. Let's turn to the Bible, and see how he set things up at the beginning.

**Read Genesis 2:5–7**

Although humankind is very much part of nature, we are not like the animals. Genesis 1 seems to say that the rest of creation was called into being through a word. Humans, though, were made by God's own hand. His fingerprints are all over us. His very breath became our breath.

Part of being made in God's image is that we have not been designed to live in isolation. God has existed for all eternity as the Trinity: a multi-faceted Godhead. One God, three persons. God has never operated solo, as we might understand it, and we were not intended to either.

**Read Genesis 2:18**

- Why do you think God said it wasn't good for Adam to be alone?

So, God let Adam loose among the creatures he'd made. He could name them, play with them, interact with them. But being a pet-lover still wasn't enough.

**Read Genesis 2:20b–23**

It seems that creation was now complete and could exist in perfect peace and harmony. But, despite the way our culture has developed, we were not created for self-sufficiency. God did not design us for doing life alone. He meant us to have the help of another and even that wasn't enough. They needed God as their constant, ever-present companion.

**Read the Genesis 3:8a**

God didn't make a helper for Adam and then leave them both to it. God was there, in the garden, eager to spend time with them when the work was done. Our need for him was in-built. He created us to live in community with our fellow humans *and* him.

Tragically, this idyll came to an abrupt end when sin entered the world.

**Read Genesis 3:6–7**

Adam and Eve grabbed whatever was to hand, to cover up their new sense of shame.

- If being weak is a shared human experience, why do we spend so much time trying to cover it up?
- What are some of the things we try to cover up with?

It's really important to understand that we are all in the same boat.

**Read Romans 3:23**

- Since we are all weakened by sin and its effects, how could we respond differently to each other? In other words, what if we all stopped the covering up and saying 'I'm fine'?

**Read James 5:16**

- How do you feel about confessing our sins to each other? Is it necessary?
- What do you think might be the benefits of doing so for us individually and corporately?

**Read Matthew 20:31–34**

- Why did Jesus have to ask them what they wanted him to do?
- In what ways can it be powerful and effective to say something out loud?
- How did Jesus respond to their honesty?

The life and ministry of Jesus centred on doing something about our weakness. He dignified the poor and the weak, and he is armed with compassion. But first we have to admit to it.

We're all in this together.

We need to model honesty in order to encourage honesty from other people.

**Response**

Write on a piece of paper one aspect of your life in which you feel weak.

Fold it up tight and pass it to the next person.

Nobody is to open the folded slip, but in holding them, it is a sign that we are here to bear each other's burdens.

Spend a few moments in silent or spoken prayer, then hand the slips back, thanking them for sharing it with you.

# Session 2
# LEARNING FROM NAOMI ABOUT REGRET, GRIEF, AND DISAPPOINTMENT

*Ask attendees to, if possible, read chapters 5, 8, 9, and 10 in advance.*

The story of Ruth, found in an Old Testament book containing only four chapters, might be familiar as a love story between the young widow and Boaz, the older 'guardian-redeemer' who rescued, then married, her. But in focusing on her mother-in-law, Naomi, we witness her struggle with bereavement and loss, regret, disappointment, and despair, and we can explore her experience of God using these 'intruders' for his own purposes: bringing hope, restoration, and renewed strength.

**Ice-breaker question:** When is the last time that someone or something disappointed you?

## Background

When famine hit Bethlehem, one family decided to uproot and move to Moab. The 50-mile walk across steep and rocky terrain would have taken around ten days to complete. Not a journey for the faint-hearted! Of course, hope proved a powerful motivator to keep going.

The move spared them from starvation, but not from fresh sorrows. Naomi, the family's matriarch, was widowed, and then lost her two sons, leaving her daughters-in-law widows, too.

Into this horror at last came some good news: the famine had lifted.

Bethlehem had food again. It was time to go home.

**Read Ruth 1:7–9**

Walking always give us opportunity to think. I doubt they had got far before Naomi realised she was asking too much from the two younger women.

**Read Ruth 1:12–13**

Naomi's first statement is obvious enough: there was no way the 'girls' could continue being her daughters-in-law. But what of her summary, 'The Lord's hand has turned against me!'?

- Why do you think she drew this conclusion?
- What other explanation could there have been?
- Have any of us ever felt or said something similar?

**Read Ruth 1:16–17**

These words are often quoted as examples of loving dedication, one to another. What, though, were the gains and the costs to her of saying them?

**Read Ruth 1:19–21**

Here, Naomi is reinforcing the strength of her disappointment. Everything has gone wrong, and it's all God's fault.

- What was the point in Naomi saying all that?
- How did it affect her circumstances?
- Is there value in us expressing raw honesty, even when it's not very nice?

Ruth 2 sees Ruth beginning to work in the fields, keeping close to the edges where grain was left specifically for the poor to glean from.

Catching the eye of the landowner, Boaz, meant that suddenly Ruth and Naomi had more to eat than they could manage.

It's the start of Ruth's happy ending, but what is there in it for Naomi? Let's look at what God did for Naomi and can do for us.

## God stirs hope in the midst of desolation

God places us in families, to be a mutual blessing to each other. Ruth's commitment to her mother-in-law brought obvious reward for herself, in finding new love, but Naomi shares in it. Sometimes, seeing God move in a loved one's life stirs hope for our own.

- What are the steps that track the progression in Naomi's situation from despair to the promise of something better?
- Is there anything here anyone can relate to?

## God gives fresh purpose

Naomi came back to Bethlehem as a broken woman, with all her dreams dashed. Perhaps as she travelled from Moab she was only thinking about where she wanted to be buried.

- In what ways did God overwrite that narrative and give her not only hope but a reason for living?
- At what point do you think Naomi started to take notice of the change in her heart?

## God can overturn what's gone before

It's likely that Naomi regretted ever leaving Bethlehem, given everything that went wrong in Moab. She voiced her complaint to God, but who knows what inner conversations she had with herself.

- Without necessarily sharing what it is, discuss the effect that regret has on our lives. Are we still living with the consequences or is God turning things around?

## God's strength replaces our weakness – and pays the blessing forward into future generations

As the credits start to roll at the end of the story, we see Naomi with a precious grandson on her lap. All her friends, old and new, share the celebration that 'Naomi has a son'. This child, Obed, would grow to have a son of his own: Jesse, the father of King David.

## Questions for further discussion

- Why do you think God lets us sink so low before help arrives?
- It might be said that Naomi interfered in trying to push Ruth and Boaz together. Do you agree? Does God ever need a helping hand?

## Response

The story of Naomi is one filled with hope and the generosity of God. However, when we are going through a tough time, it is hard to imagine something so good happening to us.

If you feel able, share with the group how things are right now. Naomi didn't bottle up how she was feeling, but told it in quite brutal terms. If it's easier to be honest in a journal, write it down once you get home.

Spend time praying for each other, and pledge to keep an eye out for 'signs of spring' that we may not notice in our own lives. Sometimes our prayers can be answered in surprising ways!

# Session 3
# LEARNING FROM ELIJAH ABOUT BURN-OUT AND ISOLATION

*Ask attendees to, if possible, read chapters 11, 12, and 13 in advance.*

We looked at the story of Naomi last time, highlighting how she suffered in the areas of regret, bereavement, and disappointment. Today we're looking at the prophet Elijah. He performed powerful exploits in God's name, but afterwards was left weak through burn-out, depression, and isolation. In many ways, his story is an extreme one, yet it demonstrates how God offered his strength in a time of crisis and stress. God wants to encourage us in similar ways, in circumstances big and small.

**Ice-breaker question:** What's the most difficult thing you've ever had to do on your own?

**Read 1 Kings 19:1–4**

## Background

Elijah is fresh from a massive victory over the prophets of Baal on Mount Carmel (1 Kings 18). Except that he's far from fresh. The experience stretched him in every way:

*Physically* – he repaired the altar of the Lord by hefting twelve stones into position. Then he dug a trench, arranged wood for a fire, butchered a bull, and laid the cuts on to the wood. He got the spectators to fill the four large jars with water, but he'd done everything up to then.

And that's before the contest even started.

*Spiritually* – this was such a public display. We don't know how many people were watching, but we know it included 450 prophets of Baal, 400 prophets of Asherah, and as many of the nation's inhabitants that decided to come. He was trusting God, for sure – but what if God didn't show up? He could have been left looking pretty stupid.

*Emotionally* – doing all this was flying in the face of the tyrannical king and queen. Queen Jezebel had his death warrant signed and sealed. He was a dead man walking. We can only imagine how he was feeling inside.

So, once this encounter was over, there was no time to relish the victory. Exhausted and terrified, he ran for his life. Burned out and desperate, he just wanted to die.

- When we're tired and worn out, how do we like to be treated?
- Is that something we need other people for, or has anyone had a sense of God coming alongside?
- Do you have an example to share?

**Read 1 Kings 19:5–9a**

This is such a tender encounter.

- Does it surprise you that God did this? Why (or why not)?

**Read Psalm 145:8, 14–15**

Note that it says 'at the proper time' (v. 15). This is just what happens here. God gives Elijah food, supernaturally sourced and delivered, at the time he needs it. He lets him sleep it off. Then repeats the process. There is no sense of rebuke here. All we are seeing is the compassion of God at work.

- Why do you think God had to treat Elijah with such care?
- What does it teach us about how we treat ourselves and each other when we're 'beyond it'?

**Read 1 Kings 19:9b–13**

- Why did you think God asked Elijah, 'What are you doing here?'
- What happens, in our own experience, when we say something out loud?
- Go through the elements of Elijah's reply. How much of what he says is actually true?

We mustn't underestimate what effect physical exhaustion can have on our perspective and, indeed, on our faith.

Let's look at how God made things better.

God gave Elijah a reminder of God's power. He'd already witnessed it on Mount Carmel, but that's before he crashed. And before, it was in front of hundreds of witnesses; here, it was just God and Elijah. Would it play out the same? Did God only do the fire 'trick' to demonstrate he was the only true God? Could/would God be powerful just for Elijah alone?

He spoke in a gentle whisper. I imagine he spoke Elijah's name. What else might he have said, do you think?

We whisper as an act of intimacy. These words are not for general consumption. I am speaking to you alone. I am drawing close to make sure you catch what I say.

Furthermore, God may have been meaning: you have seen my power but what you *need* is my intimacy – and that's your source of strength.

**Read 1 Kings 19:14–16**

This can read as if Elijah had rehearsed his speech, as the prodigal son did on his journey home.

- In summary, what are all the ways in which Elijah received strength from God?
- Is there one which 'did the trick', or was it the combination of them all that was most effective?

## Response

So often, we play down (even to ourselves) how we are feeling, saying things like: 'I'm just a bit tired.' When that goes on for too long, we become susceptible to overwhelm.

If members of the group are comfortable doing so, share honestly how things are going.

Is there something practical we can offer each other? A burden we can carry together?

Bring it all to God in prayer, praying out loud altogether can be uplifting, both in the doing and the hearing!

Elijah felt that he was all alone, which compounded his desperation. We have each other. How can we best express that this week?

# Session 4

# GOD IS OUR REFUGE AND IS STRONG, THROUGH AND THROUGH

*Ask attendees to, if possible, read chapters 20 and 21 in advance.*

We've been looking so far at our own weakness, and how some people in the Bible came through difficult situations with God's help. It's time to turn our focus on to God, the ultimate example of what 'strong' looks like, and the source of our strength.

**Ice-breaker questions:** Have you ever been caught in a storm? Where did you shelter?

God's strength is too great for us to understand, so the Bible relies on many metaphors and comparisons to try to convey it. We're going to concentrate on two aspects: God is a refuge and strong tower, and God is strong through and through.

## God is a refuge and strong tower

**Read Psalm 61:3 and 2 Samuel 22:3**

- How do you picture this refuge / strong tower / stronghold?
- Where is it on the landscape?
- Does it say 'Keep away' or 'Come near'?

When applied to God, this tower always has a welcome: the righteous can run to it, find shelter there, and be protected from the storm.

**Read Psalm 91:1–4**

- How do these verses develop the idea of God being a refuge?
- What do you make of its tender description?
- Is this something anyone has experienced that they can share?

## God is strong, through and through

We know from our dealings with others that some people are safe for us through aspects of their character. God ticks every box when it comes to how good, reliable, and trustworthy he is.

**God is eternal – read Psalm 90:2**

- What are the implications of God being eternal?
- How does him being so become a source of strength for us?

**God will never leave us – read Deuteronomy 31:6**

This is a significant part of his strength. When we've lost connection with people, for whatever reason, that rift can weaken us and leave us feeling 'less than' for a while. We never need to experience that with God.

- Do you have a testimony of knowing God was with you at a difficult time?
- How did you know he was present?

**God is faithful – read Deuteronomy 7:9**

This verse comes early in the Bible, when relatively few generations had known God or walked with him. But they had already worked out and knew for certain that God is faithful.

- How does God's faithfulness play out in your life?
- Do the stories of other people finding God faithful help you, or do you think it is something we can only find out for ourselves?

**God is unchanging – read Malachi 3:6**

- Is reliability the same as faithfulness?
- How is God's unchanging nature a source of strength to us?

**God is good – read Psalm 25:8**

- What security do we derive from knowing that God is always good, all the time?

## Response

As we think about the amazing attributes of God, remember that this information only helps us if it moves from our heads into our hearts.

We will never reach God's perfection, but we are called to become more and more like him.

Write down privately which aspect particularly challenged you today. Is it an area you need to trust God more in? Or is it a quality that's lacking in your own life?

Pray for each other to come into a fuller appreciation of God's strength and for him to help us as we play our part in helping those around us.

## Session 5

# HOW TO STRENGTHEN OURSELVES IN THE LORD: LEARNING FROM DAVID

*Ask attendees to, if possible, read chapter 22 in advance.*

Some years ago, I was on the final day of Wainwright's coast-to-coast walk and hit a problem: a deep and wide area of bog ahead. My friends were already ahead, waiting for me. I was stuck. Whichever way I looked, there was no obvious (dry or easy) place to tread on. I called across to my friends: 'How did you get over there?'

This is the burning question: if we are weak and God is strong, how do we access that strength for ourselves?

**Ice-breaker question:** Can you recall a time when someone gave you a (literal) helping hand?

We're looking this time at an episode in the life of David. King Saul is consumed with jealousy and is hunting David down to kill him. David previously soothed the king's moods by playing his harp, but has had to flee to Philistine territory (Israel's sworn enemies) to escape Saul's reach. There, David continues to be a valiant warrior.

By chapter 29, thousands of Philistine troops are about to go to war against the Israelites, at which point David's loyalty is called into question. King Achish therefore sends David back to his home town of Ziklag.

**Read 1 Samuel 30:1–6**

Note this phrase: 'But David found strength in the Lord his God.' (The ESV has it as: 'But David strengthened himself in the Lord his God.')

The passage doesn't tell us how David did so, but we do know he wrote many of the Psalms. We can draw on their pattern, as well as learn from what they reveal about his relationship with God.

- What do you think David had learned from those times soothing Saul with his harp-playing? (What kind of music do you imagine it was?)
- Is there an equivalent for us?
- How many of us use Psalms in our devotional times? What is it about them that is so helpful?
- Do you think writing different psalms strengthened David, or did they flow out of the strength he'd already received from God?

There isn't a specific psalm that connects with the incident at Ziklag, but Psalm 62 offers a typical pattern for seeking God in crisis that we can follow.

**Read Psalm 62:1–2**

- How is the way this starts so important?

**Read Psalm 62:3–4**

- What do you notice about the way David describes his situation?

**Read Psalm 62:5–8**

- Who is David addressing here?
- How is this helpful?
- What does focussing on God's attributes achieve?

**Read Psalm 62:9–10**

- What has David's fresh perspective enabled him to see?

**Read Psalm 62:11–12**

- How does the psalm finish, and why is this important?
- Why is it important to be honest with God about how we're feeling?
- How can we develop that same honesty with each other?
- Can you think of a time when you have consciously praised God when you haven't felt like it or when life was particularly hard?
- What effect did it have?
- Does it get easier, the more you do it?
- What does 'resting in God' mean?
- How does resting restore us, body, mind, and soul?

## Conclusion

David's story highlights some good lessons we can learn from:

Make sure we're in the right place. When we're not, it affects our thinking, our faith, and our actions.

We need to submit to God, surrender our own agenda, and acknowledge him as as Lord. We must listen to him and obey what he says.

## Response

Spend some time in twos or threes, sharing briefly what needs you have, then praying for each other to know God's strength in a real way.

During the coming week, try writing your own psalm and be ready to share it next time.

## Session 6

# THE PRIME IMPORTANCE OF CONNECTION

*Ask attendees to, if possible, read chapters 23 and 24 in advance.*

We were never designed to live independent, self-sufficient lives. We owe our very existence to our connection and communion with God. This sense of connection goes both ways: we must keep hold of some things, and God keeps hold of us. He has no direct need of us – other than to satisfy his love and his good pleasure in creating us – but we have a deep, craving need of him. It's not just about plugging into his strength. It's about our very survival.

**Ice-breaker question:** If you were in danger, what would you prefer: something to grab hold of or someone to grab hold of you?

## Connection

**Read John 15:4–6**

I had such a vivid demonstration of these verses when one of our youth workers came into a meeting carrying a freshly cut vine stem. After we'd worshipped and shared, she spoke briefly on the importance of connection with God, then I reached down to pick the stem up for her. In such a short space of time, it was flaccid, hanging from my fingers like no more than a piece of rope.

- How does this image relate to Jesus' teaching about him being the vine?
- Is he speaking literally, do you think? Why?

- Is it enough to connect with other believers, even if we neglect our personal devotional times?
- Or, conversely, do you find that you don't need fellowship with others if your relationship with Jesus is close?

**Read Hebrews 10:24–25**

It is never a question of just ticking off 'Go to church' in our diaries.

- What benefits and blessings in meeting together does the writer both state and imply here?
- Are we ever tempted to skip the Sunday service, the midweek fellowship, or the prayer meeting? What happens when we do?

**Read 1 John 1:7–8**

There is an implication of accountability here.

- How important is our connection with each other when it comes to the Christian life?

The Bible makes it clear that the choice is a stark one: when we are disconnected from the vine, we are as good as dead. Nor can we do without each other, no matter how difficult that can be sometimes!

## Holding on

The second aspect of connection is found in the Bible's teaching that there are some things we need to let go of, such as sinful habits, and other things we have to take hold of. If you've ever been to a party where you're holding a paper plate full of food in one hand and a glass of drink in the other, you will know how difficult it is to actually eat anything – never mind greet the person coming up to you. Likewise, we cannot take hold of the things of God while still persisting in grasping the 'old stuff'.

**Read Proverbs 4:13 and 2 Thessalonians 2:15**

- How can we do this as individuals?
- How can we encourage each other to do so?

**Read Philippians 2:16**

- Does anyone have a testimony to share about how holding on to God's word helped you?
- Is there a particular verse or promise you repeat to yourself?
- Has a passage 'leapt off the page' recently and addressed a situation you'd been praying over?

## Being held

God is not a God who is strong but distant.

His strength does not need to be imagined or conjured up or, for that matter, reached out for, as if it's too far away. 'God did this so that they would seek him and perhaps reach out for him and find him, though he is not far from any one of us' (Acts 17:27).

God is near. He is within touching distance. We are held within his embrace.

**Read Psalm 91:4–5**

These verses follow on from the ones viewing God as a refuge and fortress that we looked at in session 4.

- How does the image of a mother bird shielding her chicks under her wings fit with the starker description of God as a fortress?
- How have you experienced this in your own life, or in that of someone you know?

## Response

Share, if you feel able, which one of the three aspects (connected to the vine/holding on/being held) resonates the most.

Which one presents the biggest challenge? Are there any practical ways we can 'spur one another on' this coming week?

Read out the psalms written in response to last week's session.

Move into a time of praise, perhaps using some of the phrases written by the group.

Spend time thanking God for each other, then praying into any needs.

# Session 7
# FINAL THOUGHTS

*Ask attendees to, if possible, read chapter 31 in advance.*

In our last session together, there are a few further thoughts to consider about how God uses our suffering and weakness and why it is so important to turn to him for our strength.

**Ice-breaker questions:** Is there a horrible situation you have faced that you can look back on and be glad you went through it? Why can you say that?

## Why do we have to face hardship?

When life is so hard, but we know we have a good God, it is perfectly reasonable to ask ourselves why we have to face such difficulties.

Discuss together some of your own opinions as to why God leads us the hard way.

When a chick is trying to hatch itself, it's tempting for us to break the shell for it, believing we're helping. However, the act of pecking is what strengthens the chick for survival. Our 'help' can actually cause the bird to die.

**Read Romans 5:2–4**

- What do these verses offer us?
- In what ways can we draw strength from this teaching?

## Helping others

The Bible makes clear that one reason we go through trials is so that we are able to empathise, comfort, and help other people when they are suffering.

**Read 2 Corinthians 1:3–4**

- Do you have a testimony about an occasion you were able to offer comfort, or receive it, in this way? How did it strengthen you?

When listening to each other's stories, it's tempting to turn the conversation around and make it about us and what we've gone through. Instead, let's show each other respect by giving our full attention.

**Read Hebrews 4:15**

- What difference does it make to you to know that God understands our weakness?

## Being honest with God and each other

**Read Psalm 6:6–7**

These kinds of details are probably ones we would hide from other people. We might dismiss how we're feeling as 'a bit this…', but since God sees and knows everything, we don't have to pretend.

How easy do you find it to tell God how things really are?

What happens when we don't admit to ourselves, God, or other people what's really going on?

## Yielding ourselves afresh to God

**Read Luke 22:41–44**

These are probably the most significant verses within the crucifixion story. Jesus (fully human, remember) had already been under intense pressure and threat and now is facing the most gruesome death. This is desperation at its most extreme. He pleads with God to spare him, but ultimately yields his will and lets God have his way. Note the detail that an angel came alongside him to strengthen him.

- How important is it that we keep ourselves submitted to God?
- What difference does it make to our weakness and suffering when we yield every aspect of our lives to him?

## Scars

We would probably prefer our strengthening and restoration to be so complete that it left no trace of what had happened. Sadly, this is not the way. Sometimes our circumstances will stay unchanged while God does an amazing job inside us. Other times, we are healed but still bear the scars.

**Read Luke 24:39–40**

- Does it surprise you that Jesus' resurrected body still showed where the nails had been?
- What significance has that got for us?
- How easy do we find it to show someone else our scars, so to speak?

**Read 2 Corinthians 12:9**

- How does this sum up all that we've been looking at through the book and discussion times?
- How does it help us?

## Response

If there is time, invite each member to share the most significant thing they have learned on the course, and what they plan to take away and keep seeking God for.

Pray for each other in twos or threes, for each person to know God's strength in increasing measure.

End by saying the grace, with our eyes open:

*May the grace of the Lord Jesus Christ, the love of God, and the fellowship of the Holy Spirit be with us all, now and evermore. Amen.*

# FURTHER READING

Liz Carter, *Catching Contentment: How to be holy satisfied* (IVP, 2018).

Sarah Clarkson, *Reclaiming Quiet: Cultivating a life of holy attention* (Baker Books, 2024).

Timothy Keller, *Forgive: Why should I and how can I?* (Hodder and Stoughton, 2022).

Pat Marsh, *Dwelling in the Psalms: A healing journey* (Kevin Mayhew, 2019).

Emily Owen, *Still Emily: Seeing rainbows in the silence* (Malcolm Down, 2016).

Jane Walters (Clamp), *Too Soon: A mother's journey through miscarriage* (SPCK, 2018).

# NOTES

1 I have shared the full story in my book (as Jane Clamp) *Too Soon: A mother's journey through miscarriage* (SPCK, 2018).
2 Hymn written by Charles Wesley (1707–88).
3 **thegospelcoalition.org/article/reflections-on-50th-anniversary-of-my-diving-accident**
4 'Joni Eareckson Tada's songs of suffering: 25 hymns and devotions for weary souls', **youtu.be/0H9ztsfGfRM**.
5 **ca.thegospelcoalition.org/article/what-is-lament-and-how-to-help-others-lament**
6 **oxfordlearnersdictionaries.com/us/definition/english/tipping-point**
7 My use of the word 'rage' here doesn't mean I was always angry, but I'm keen to emphasise that anger is far better out than in. Denying we are angry only causes more problems later. Expressing it carefully and without injuring others is important.
8 **churchtimes.co.uk/articles/2017/24-november/features/features/fed-by-grit-and-the-prayer-book**
9 **oed.com/dictionary/abide_v**
10 **psychologytoday.com/us/blog/possibilitizing/202501/finding-joy-when-the-world-feels-heavy**
11 'Theology of suffering – Joni Eareckson Tada', **youtu.be/ejbHemlrbU4**.